THIS BOOK BELONGS TO

_____

START DATE

_____

SHE READS TRUTH

FOUNDERS

FOUNDER
Raechel Myers

CO-FOUNDER
Amanda Bible Williams

EXECUTIVE

CHIEF EXECUTIVE OFFICER
Ryan Myers

CHIEF OPERATING OFFICER
Mark D. Bullard

EDITORIAL

MANAGING EDITOR
Lindsey Jacobi, MDiv

PRODUCTION EDITOR
Hannah Little, MTS

ASSOCIATE EDITOR
Kayla De La Torre, MAT

COPY EDITOR
Becca Owens, MA

CREATIVE

SENIOR ART DIRECTOR
Annie Glover

DESIGN MANAGER
Kelsea Allen

DESIGNERS
Savannah Ault
Ashley Phillips

MARKETING

MARKETING DIRECTOR
Whitney Hoffmann

GROWTH MARKETING MANAGERS
Katie Bevels
Blake Showalter

PRODUCT MARKETING MANAGER
Krista Squibb

CONTENT MARKETING STRATEGIST
Tameshia Williams, ThM

MARKETING SPECIALIST
Bailey Majewski

OPERATIONS

OPERATIONS DIRECTOR
Allison Sutton

OPERATIONS MANAGER
Mary Beth Steed

GROUP SALES AND
ENGAGEMENT SPECIALIST
Karson Speth

OPERATIONS ASSISTANT
Emily Andrews

SHIPPING

SHIPPING MANAGER
Marian Welch

FULFILLMENT LEAD
Kajsa Matheny

FULFILLMENT SPECIALISTS
Hannah Lamb
Kelsey Simpson

COMMUNITY ENGAGEMENT

COMMUNITY ENGAGEMENT MANAGER
Delaney Coleman

COMMUNITY ENGAGEMENT SPECIALISTS
Cait Baggerman
Katy McKnight
Heather Vollono

CONTRIBUTORS

RECIPE
Rebekah Barnes (94)

SPECIAL THANKS
Abbey Benson
Lauren Haag

SUBSCRIPTION INQUIRIES
orders@shereadstruth.com

SHE READS TRUTH™

© 2024 by She Reads Truth, LLC
All rights reserved.

All photography used by permission.

ISBN 978-1-962221-15-3

1 2 3 4 5 6 7 8 9 10

@SHEREADSTRUTH

Download the She Reads Truth app, available for iOS and Android

Subscribe to the She Reads Truth Podcast

This book was printed offset in Nashville, Tennessee, on 70# Lynx Opaque. Cover is Neenah Eggshell 80#C in Avalanche White.

ADVENT 2024

THE DAWN OF REDEEMING GRACE

SHE READS TRUTH

LET US READ GOD'S PROMISES
TOGETHER, ANCHORED BY
THE JOY OF CELEBRATING
THE COMING DAWN.

Raechel Myers
FOUNDER

"It's always darkest before dawn."

To be honest, this saying has always bugged me. I'm not trying to be difficult or a know-it-all, but it's just not scientifically true. Step outside on any given night and you'll find that darkness throughout the night changes depending on cloud movement or the moon. In the winter months, light can be affected if something like snow is reflecting the light. So why do we use this not-exactly-true saying to comfort one another?

I suppose the breathtaking break of the morning sun across the horizon does make everything in the hours before seem much darker. So maybe that's why? Or maybe it just feels really good and hopeful? But what I've learned is that the almost-true things are never nearly as comforting as the absolutely-true things.

When I learned that this year's Advent reading plan was titled *The Dawn of Redeeming Grace*, my soul gave a sigh of relief at the thought. I imagine the world did seem darker than ever before that dawn—the birth of the Messiah. It probably seemed like hope, peace, joy, and love were growing dimmer by the day. But the truer truth is this: God was always at work. His promises to the prophets, priests, kings, and everyday people were still true, even though they couldn't see the Light waiting to be revealed at the perfect time.

Of all of the things I love about our Advent journey this year, what I hope you connect with deeply is the Old Testament scriptures and the eager anticipation of knowing that the Light has, in fact, dawned. As for this Christmas season, when things may seem dark and we need to be reminded of why we have peace and hope and joy, why we love and rejoice in the good news, let us read God's promises together, anchored by the joy of celebrating the coming dawn. Even though we can't see Him, we know He is at work. "Look, I am coming soon!" (Revelation 22:7).

Friends, don't miss this Advent season. I want to personally invite you to make time to open these Advent scriptures every single day. Let God's Word be a lamp to your feet and a light to your path (Psalm 119:105). This way, whether things seem dark now or even when they inevitably will, you will know that the Light, who came into the world at the first advent, will most certainly return once and for all. Together, let's let our souls sigh with sweet relief.

DESIGN
ON
PURPOSE

At She Reads Truth, we believe in pairing the inherently beautiful Word of God with the aesthetic beauty it deserves. Each of our resources is thoughtfully and artfully designed to highlight the beauty, goodness, and truth of Scripture in a way that reflects the themes of each curated reading plan.

One of the central inspirations for this year's Advent design comes from our key verse, John 1:14, which says, "And the Word became flesh and dwelt among us, and we have seen his glory, glory as of the only Son from the Father, full of grace and truth." The fullness of God wrapped in human flesh so that He might dwell with us reminded us of the delicate, intricate details in antique lace. Illustrated candles throughout this book point us to the traditional themes of the Advent candles, which will guide our reading. The combination of these illustrations and the lace patterns create a sense of home, warmth, and reverence.

Photos of crisp snowy mornings are scattered throughout this book, bringing to mind the redeeming grace that has dawned in the middle of humanity's dark winter. These images, paired with the cursive font and modern serif you see throughout, feel both invitational and intentional as we move through this season of hope and anticipation.

HOW TO USE THIS BOOK

She Reads Truth is a community of women dedicated to reading the Word of God every day. In this **Advent 2024** reading plan, we will read passages that demonstrate what Jesus Christ, the Son of God, came to accomplish.

READ & REFLECT

Your **Advent 2024** book focuses primarily on Scripture, with added features to come alongside your time with God's Word.

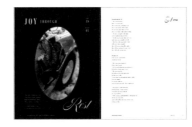

SCRIPTURE READING

Designed for a Sunday start, this book presents daily Scripture readings for the Advent season.

RESPONSE

Each weekday features space for personal reflection and prayer.

COMMUNITY & CONVERSATION

You can start reading this book at any time! If you want to join women from Flagstaff to Finland as they read along with you, the She Reads Truth community will start Day 1 of **Advent 2024** on Sunday, December 1, 2024.

 ## SHE READS TRUTH APP

Devotionals corresponding to each daily reading can be found in the **Advent 2024** reading plan on the She Reads Truth app. New devotionals will be published each weekday once the plan begins on Sunday, December 1, 2024. You can use the app to participate in community discussion and more.

GRACE DAY

Use Saturdays to catch up on your reading, pray, and rest in the presence of the Lord.

SUNDAYS

Each Sunday marks a new theme to guide your week's readings.

EXTRAS

This book features additional tools to help you gain a deeper understanding of the text.

Find a complete list of extras on page 13.

 SHEREADSTRUTH.COM

The **Advent 2024** reading plan and devotionals will also be available at SheReadsTruth.com as the community reads each day. Invite your family, friends, and neighbors to read along with you!

 SHE READS TRUTH PODCAST

Subscribe to the She Reads Truth Podcast, and join our founders and their guests each week as they talk about what you'll read in the week ahead.

 Podcast episodes 254–258 for our **Advent 2024** *series release on Mondays beginning December 2, 2024.*

TABLE OF

Contents

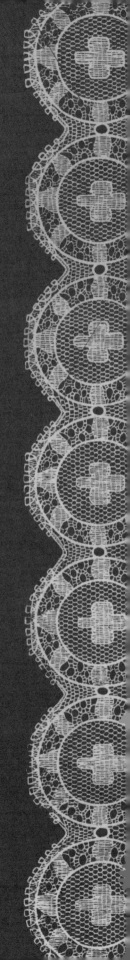

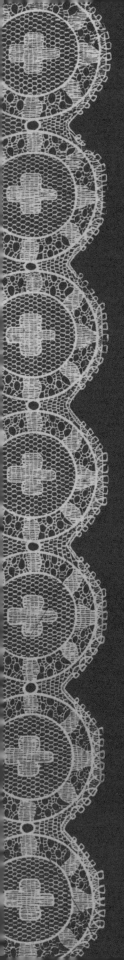

Extras

INTRODUCTION

TO

ADVENT

KEY VERSE   (JOHN 1:14)

THE WORD BECAME FLESH AND DWELT
AMONG US. WE OBSERVED HIS GLORY, THE
GLORY AS THE ONE AND ONLY SON FROM
THE FATHER, FULL OF GRACE AND TRUTH.

WHAT IS ADVENT?

Advent is a Latin word that means "coming" or "arrival." On the Church calendar, the season of Advent begins four Sundays before Christmas Day and culminates on Christmas Eve. It is a season full of expectation, longing, and hope.

Since the fourth century, Christians have observed Advent as a time to remember Jesus's first advent (His coming as a baby born in Bethlehem) and anticipate His second advent (His triumphant, future return).

TRADITION OF THE ADVENT CANDLES

Advent candles originated in the early 1800s when Johann Hinrich Wichern, a minister in Germany, created the first Advent wreath from an old cart wheel to give the children in his ministry a way to count down the days until Christmas. Red candles were lit throughout the week, and four white candles were lit each Sunday during Advent.

Many Christians now mark the four Sundays during Advent by lighting one candle each Sunday, with a fifth candle on Christmas Eve. The colors of these candles vary among denominations, but many Protestant traditions use three purple or blue candles, one pink candle, and one white candle. The purple or blue candles represent the themes of hope, peace, and love. The pink candle represents the theme of joy, and the white candle represents the light and life of Christ.

THIS ADVENT READING PLAN

For our journey, the four traditional themes of the Advent candles will guide our study. Centered around each of these themes, we will read passages that highlight what Jesus Christ, the Son of God, came to accomplish. Each Sunday introduces the theme ahead of that week's readings.

In Week 1, we'll explore how Jesus brings **hope** to a weary world.
In Week 2, we'll explore how Jesus brings **peace** to our brokenness.
In Week 3, we'll explore how Jesus brings **joy** through His life, death, and resurrection.
In Week 4, we'll explore how Jesus is **love** in the flesh.
In Week 5, we'll **rejoice** in who Jesus is and what He has done.

Holiday CALENDAR

SUNDAY	MONDAY	TUESDAY	WEDNESDAY	THURSDAY
DEC 1 ═══ FIRST SUNDAY OF ADVENT	2	3	4 Scan the QR code for a playlist with our team's favorite holiday tunes.	5
8 ═══ SECOND SUNDAY OF ADVENT	9	10	11 **DON'T FORGET!** Last day to order gifts from ShopSheReadsTruth.com with standard shipping for Christmas delivery.	12
15 ═══ THIRD SUNDAY OF ADVENT	16	17	18 Last day to order your *Genesis* Reading Guide to start reading on January 6!	19
22 ═══ FOURTH SUNDAY OF ADVENT	23 Get ahead on your Christmas morning cooking with our breakfast casserole recipe on p. 94.	24 *Christmas Eve*	25 *Christmas Day* *Christmastide begins*	26 Use the questions on p. 125 to reflect on Christmas Day.
29 ═══ FIRST SUNDAY OF CHRISTMASTIDE	30 **FOR THE RECORD** Turn to p. 148 to recap your year in the Word and pray for the year ahead!	31	JAN 1 *Happy New Year!*	2
5 ═══ SECOND SUNDAY OF CHRISTMASTIDE	Fill in your calendar with any holiday parties, to-do's, or special trips you want to remember this year!			

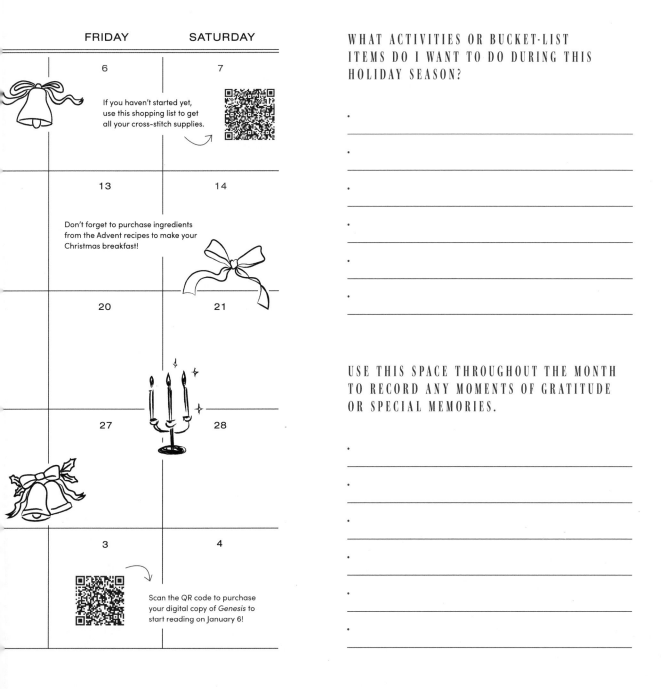

FRIDAY	SATURDAY
6	7
If you haven't started yet, use this shopping list to get all your cross-stitch supplies.	
13	14
Don't forget to purchase ingredients from the Advent recipes to make your Christmas breakfast!	
20	21
27	28
3	4
Scan the QR code to purchase your digital copy of *Genesis* to start reading on January 6!	

WHAT ACTIVITIES OR BUCKET-LIST ITEMS DO I WANT TO DO DURING THIS HOLIDAY SEASON?

- _____
- _____
- _____
- _____
- _____
- _____

USE THIS SPACE THROUGHOUT THE MONTH TO RECORD ANY MOMENTS OF GRATITUDE OR SPECIAL MEMORIES.

- _____
- _____
- _____
- _____
- _____
- _____

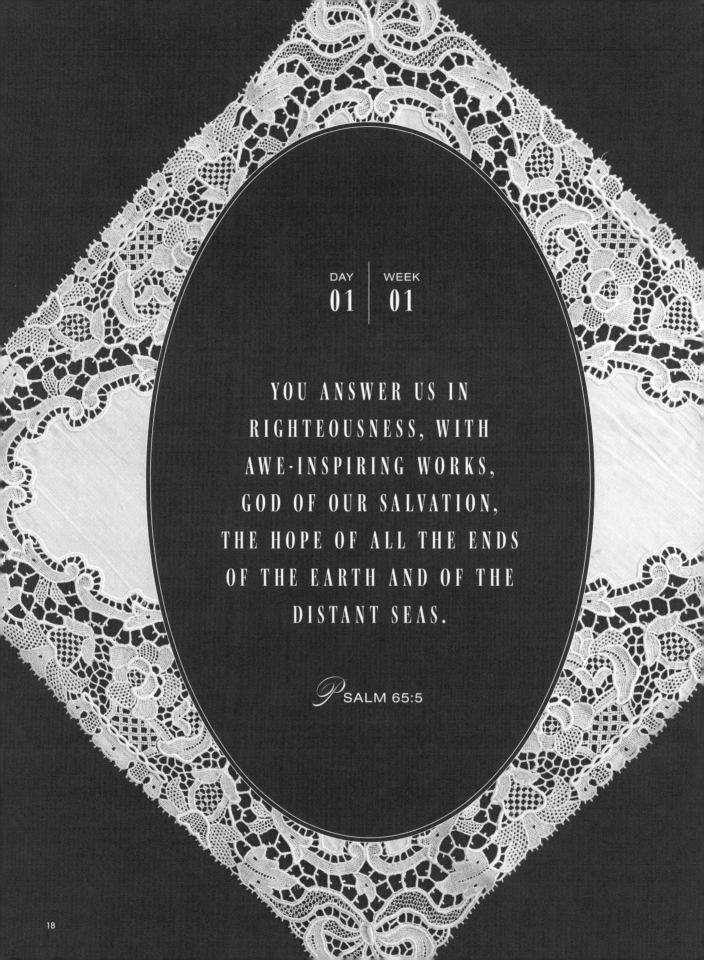

DAY | WEEK
01 | 01

YOU ANSWER US IN
RIGHTEOUSNESS, WITH
AWE-INSPIRING WORKS,
GOD OF OUR SALVATION,
THE HOPE OF ALL THE ENDS
OF THE EARTH AND OF THE
DISTANT SEAS.

*P*SALM 65:5

THE
FIRST SUNDAY
OF
ADVENT:

Hope

Hope is the expectation or desire for something beyond our current reality. We begin the Advent journey each year by reorienting our hearts to the hope of our faith: Jesus, the Messiah, the Son of God. There are many areas of life where we hope in the unseen, but when we look at Jesus—who He is and what He has accomplished—we see that we have true hope in the perfect, holy, and wonderful Savior who came to dwell on earth with us. In this week's readings, we will look at some of the specific ways that Jesus came as the hope for a weary world.

The title of each day of reading this week completes the statement
"Jesus brings..."

Hope

DAY   IN THE   02

Darkness

The true light that gives light to
everyone was coming into the world.

John 1:9

Isaiah 60:1–3, 19–22

THE LORD'S GLORY IN ZION

NOTES

1 Arise, shine, for your light has come,

and the glory of the Lord shines over you.

2 For look, darkness will cover the earth,

and total darkness the peoples;

but the Lord will shine over you,

and his glory will appear over you.

3 Nations will come to your light,

and kings to your shining brightness.

…

19 The sun will no longer be your light by day,

and the brightness of the moon will not shine on you.

The Lord will be your everlasting light,

and your God will be your splendor.

20 Your sun will no longer set,

and your moon will not fade;

for the Lord will be your everlasting light,

and the days of your sorrow will be over.

21 All your people will be righteous;

they will possess the land forever;

they are the branch I planted,

the work of my hands,

so that I may be glorified.

22 The least will become a thousand,

the smallest a mighty nation.

I am the Lord;

I will accomplish it quickly in its time.

John 1:1–9

PROLOGUE

1 In the beginning was the Word, and the Word was with God, and the Word was God. 2 He was with God in the beginning. 3 All things were created through him, and apart from him not one thing was created that has been created. 4 In him was life, and that life was the light of men. 5 That light shines in the darkness, and yet the darkness did not overcome it.

6 There was a man sent from God whose name was John. 7 He came as a witness to testify about the light, so that all might believe through him. 8 He was not the light, but he came to testify about the light. 9 The true light that gives light to everyone was coming into the world.

Matthew 4:12–16
MINISTRY IN GALILEE

[12] When he heard that John had been arrested, he withdrew into Galilee. [13] He left Nazareth and went to live in Capernaum by the sea, in the region of Zebulun and Naphtali. [14] This was to fulfill what was spoken through the prophet Isaiah:

[15] Land of Zebulun and land of Naphtali,
along the road by the sea, beyond the Jordan,
Galilee of the Gentiles.

[16] The people who live in darkness have seen a great light,

and for those living in the land of the shadow of death,
a light has dawned.

2 Corinthians 4:6

For God who said, "Let light shine out of darkness," has shone in our hearts to give the light of the knowledge of God's glory in the face of Jesus Christ.

Revelation 21:23–27

[23] The city does not need the sun or the moon to shine on it, because the glory of God illuminates it, and its lamp is the Lamb. [24] The nations will walk by its light, and the kings of the earth will bring their glory into it. [25] Its gates will never close by day because it will never be night there. [26] They will bring the glory and honor of the nations into it. [27] Nothing unclean will ever enter it, nor anyone who does what is detestable or false, but only those written in the Lamb's book of life.

DAY 02

RESPONSE

As you respond this week, consider praying about how each day's reading leads you to praise, shapes your perspective on what it means to hope, and equips you to encourage those in your community.

JESUS BRINGS HOPE IN THE DARKNESS. WRITE A PRAYER OF GRATITUDE, THANKING HIM FOR BRINGING LIGHT INTO OUR DARK WORLD.

Hope

Hope FOR HUMANITY

DAY

03

WEEK

01

For just as through one man's disobedience the many were made sinners,
so also through the one man's obedience the many will be made righteous.

Romans 5:19

Genesis 3:1–10

THE TEMPTATION AND THE FALL

1 Now the serpent was the most cunning of all the wild animals that the LORD God had made. He said to the woman, "Did God really say, 'You can't eat from any tree in the garden'?"

2 The woman said to the serpent, "We may eat the fruit from the trees in the garden. 3 But about the fruit of the tree in the middle of the garden, God said, 'You must not eat it or touch it, or you will die.'"

4 "No! You will certainly not die," the serpent said to the woman. 5 "In fact, God knows that when you eat it your eyes will be opened and you will be like God, knowing good and evil." 6 The woman saw that the tree was good for food and delightful to look at, and that it was desirable for obtaining wisdom. So she took some of its fruit and ate it; she also gave some to her husband, who was with her, and he ate it. 7 Then the eyes of both of them were opened, and they knew they were naked; so they sewed fig leaves together and made coverings for themselves.

SIN'S CONSEQUENCES

8 Then the man and his wife heard the sound of the LORD God walking in the garden at the time of the evening breeze, and they hid from the LORD God among the trees of the garden. 9 So the LORD God called out to the man and said to him, "Where are you?"

10 And he said, "I heard you in the garden, and I was afraid because I was naked, so I hid."

Matthew 4:1–11

THE TEMPTATION OF JESUS

1 Then Jesus was led up by the Spirit into the wilderness to be tempted by the devil. 2 After he had fasted forty days and forty nights, he was hungry. 3 Then the tempter approached him and said, "If you are the Son of God, tell these stones to become bread."

4 He answered, "It is written: Man must not live on bread alone but on every word that comes from the mouth of God."

5 Then the devil took him to the holy city, had him stand on the pinnacle of the temple, 6 and said to him, "If you are the Son of God, throw yourself down. For it is written:

He will give his angels orders concerning you,
and they will support you with their hands
so that you will not strike
your foot against a stone."

7 Jesus told him, "It is also written: Do not test the Lord your God."

8 Again, the devil took him to a very high mountain and showed him all the kingdoms of the world and their splendor. 9 And he said to him, "I will give you all these things if you will fall down and worship me."

10 Then Jesus told him, "Go away, Satan! For it is written: Worship the Lord your God, and serve only him."

11 Then the devil left him, and angels came and began to serve him.

Romans 5:12–21

DEATH THROUGH ADAM AND LIFE THROUGH CHRIST

12 Therefore, just as sin entered the world through one man, and death through sin, in this way death spread to all people, because all sinned. 13 In fact, sin was in the world before the law, but sin is not charged to a person's account when there is no law. 14 Nevertheless, death reigned from Adam to Moses, even over those who did not sin in the likeness of Adam's transgression. He is a type of the Coming One.

15 But the gift is not like the trespass. For if by the one man's trespass the many died, how much more have the grace of

God and the gift which comes through the grace of the one man Jesus Christ overflowed to the many. [16] And the gift is not like the one man's sin, because from one sin came the judgment, resulting in condemnation, but from many trespasses came the gift, resulting in justification. [17] If by the one man's trespass, death reigned through that one man, how much more will those who receive the overflow of grace and the gift of righteousness reign in life through the one man, Jesus Christ.

[18] So then, as through one trespass there is condemnation for everyone, so also through one righteous act there is justification leading to life for everyone. [19] For just as through one man's disobedience the many were made sinners, so also through the one man's obedience the many will be made righteous. [20] The law came along to multiply the trespass. But where sin multiplied, grace multiplied even more [21] so that, just as sin reigned in death, so also grace will reign through righteousness, resulting in eternal life through Jesus Christ our Lord.

1 Corinthians 15:45–49

[45] So it is written, The first man Adam became a living being; the last Adam became a life-giving spirit. [46] However, the spiritual is not first, but the natural, then the spiritual.

[47] The first man was from the earth, a man of dust; the second man is from heaven.

[48] Like the man of dust, so are those who are of the dust; like the man of heaven, so are those who are of heaven. [49] And just as we have borne the image of the man of dust, we will also bear the image of the man of heaven.

RESPONSE

TIME

DATE

JESUS BRINGS HOPE FOR HUMANITY. WRITE A PRAYER OF GRATITUDE,
THANKING HIM FOR DOING WHAT ADAM COULD NOT.

Hope

THE *Seasons* OF THE *Church*

Advent is just one season of the Church calendar, a centuries-old way many Christian denominations order the year to remember and celebrate the redeeming work of Christ. Structured around the moving date of Easter Sunday and the fixed date of Christmas, the liturgical Church calendar consists of six seasons as well as ordinary time.

ADVENT

WHAT IS IT?
Advent is a season anticipating both the celebration of Jesus's birth as well as His promised return. The term *advent* comes from a Latin word meaning "coming" or "arrival."

WHEN IS IT?
Advent begins four Sundays before Christmas Day and runs through December 24.

CHRISTMASTIDE

WHAT IS IT?
It is a season celebrating the birth of Jesus.

WHEN IS IT?
Christmastide is from December 25 to January 5, also known as the Twelve Days of Christmas and Yuletide.

KEY SCRIPTURES
Is 9:2–7; Mt 1:18–25; Lk 1:26–38; 2:1–20

EPIPHANY

WHAT IS IT?
Epiphany comes from a Greek word that means "to manifest" or "to show." It is also known as the Feast of the Three Kings, Three Kings' Day, and Twelfth Night. Epiphany commemorates the arrival of the wise men and is a reminder that Christ's birth is good news for all creation.

WHEN IS IT?
Epiphany is on January 6, twelve days after Christmas. Some traditions celebrate this as a season through the Sunday before Ash Wednesday rather than as just one day.

KEY SCRIPTURE
Mt 2:1–12

LENT

WHAT IS IT?   Lent is a solemn season of self-reflection, repentance, and Scripture meditation as a means of preparing one's heart and mind to celebrate Easter.

WHEN IS IT?   Lent begins on Ash Wednesday and continues through Holy Saturday, consisting of forty fasting days and six feasting Sundays.

KEY SCRIPTURE   Lk 4:1–13

EASTERTIDE

WHAT IS IT?   It is a celebration of Jesus Christ's resurrection, the central belief of the Christian faith. Eastertide is the culmination of Lent.

WHEN IS IT?   Easter Sunday begins Eastertide, and it lasts through the day before Pentecost. At seven weeks, it is the longest formal season of the Church year.

KEY SCRIPTURES   Lk 24:1–12, 36–53; Jn 11:25–26

PENTECOST

WHAT IS IT?   Pentecost is a celebration of when the Holy Spirit descended on believers from all over the world who were gathered in Jerusalem. It marks the birth of the Christian Church.

WHEN IS IT?   It is the seventh Sunday after Easter.

KEY SCRIPTURE   Ac 2:1–41

ORDINARY TIME

Most of the Church calendar consists of ordinary time, the periods between Pentecost and Advent, and Epiphany and Lent.

Hope FOR THE *Nations*

Genesis 12:1–3

THE CALL OF ABRAM

[1] The LORD said to Abram:

Go from your land,
your relatives,
and your father's house
to the land that I will show you.
[2] I will make you into a great nation,
I will bless you,
I will make your name great,
and you will be a blessing.
[3] I will bless those who bless you,
I will curse anyone who treats you with contempt,
and all the peoples on earth
will be blessed through you.

Psalm 65:5

You answer us in righteousness,
with awe-inspiring works,
God of our salvation,
the hope of all the ends of the earth
and of the distant seas.

Acts 3:17–25

[17] And now, brothers and sisters, I know that you acted in ignorance, just as your leaders also did. [18] In this way God fulfilled what he had predicted through all the prophets—that his Messiah would suffer. [19] Therefore repent and turn back, so that your sins may be wiped out, [20] that seasons of refreshing may come from the presence of the Lord, and that he may send Jesus, who has been appointed for you as the

Messiah. [21] Heaven must receive him until the time of the restoration of all things, which God spoke about through his holy prophets from the beginning. [22] Moses said: The Lord your God will raise up for you a prophet like me from among your brothers. You must listen to everything he tells you. [23] And everyone who does not listen to that prophet will be completely cut off from the people.

[24] In addition, all the prophets who have spoken, from Samuel and those after him, have also foretold these days. [25] You are the sons of the prophets and of the covenant that God made with your ancestors, saying to Abraham, And all the families of the earth will be blessed through your offspring.

Galatians 3:7-29

[7] You know, then, that those who have faith, these are Abraham's sons.

[8] Now the Scripture saw in advance that God would justify the Gentiles by faith and proclaimed the gospel ahead of time to Abraham, saying, All the nations will be blessed through you.

[9] Consequently, those who have faith are blessed with Abraham, who had faith.

LAW AND PROMISE

[10] For all who rely on the works of the law are under a curse, because it is written, Everyone who does not do everything written in the book of the law is cursed. [11] Now it is clear that no one is justified before God by the law, because the righteous will live by faith. [12] But the law is not based on faith; instead, the one who does these things will live by them. [13] Christ redeemed us from the curse of the law by becoming a curse for us, because it is written, Cursed is everyone who is hung on a tree. [14] The purpose was that the blessing of Abraham would come to the Gentiles by Christ Jesus, so that we could receive the promised Spirit through faith.

[15] Brothers and sisters, I'm using a human illustration. No one sets aside or makes additions to a validated human will. [16] Now the promises were spoken to Abraham and to his seed. He does not say "and to seeds," as though referring to many, but referring to one, and to your seed, who is Christ. [17] My point is this: The law, which came 430 years later, does not invalidate a covenant previously established by God and thus cancel the promise. [18] For if the inheritance is based on the law, it is no longer based on the promise; but God has graciously given it to Abraham through the promise.

THE PURPOSE OF THE LAW

[19] Why, then, was the law given? It was added for the sake of transgressions until the Seed to whom the promise was made would come. The law was put into effect through angels by means of a mediator. [20] Now a mediator is not just for one person alone, but God is one. [21] Is the law therefore contrary to God's promises? Absolutely not! For if the law had been granted with the ability to give life, then righteousness would certainly be on the basis of the law. [22] But the Scripture imprisoned everything under sin's power, so that the promise might be given on the basis of faith in Jesus Christ to those who believe. [23] Before this faith came, we were confined under the law, imprisoned until the coming faith was revealed. [24] The law, then, was our guardian until Christ, so that we could be justified by faith. [25] But since that faith has come, we are no longer under a guardian, [26] for through faith you are all sons of God in Christ Jesus.

SONS AND HEIRS

[27] For those of you who were baptized into Christ have been clothed with Christ. [28] There is no Jew or Greek, slave or free, male and female; since you are all one in Christ Jesus. [29] And if you belong to Christ, then you are Abraham's seed, heirs according to the promise.

JESUS BRINGS HOPE FOR THE NATIONS. WRITE A PRAYER OF GRATITUDE, THANKING HIM FOR MAKING A WAY FOR THE WHOLE WORLD TO EXPERIENCE HIS BLESSING.

Hope

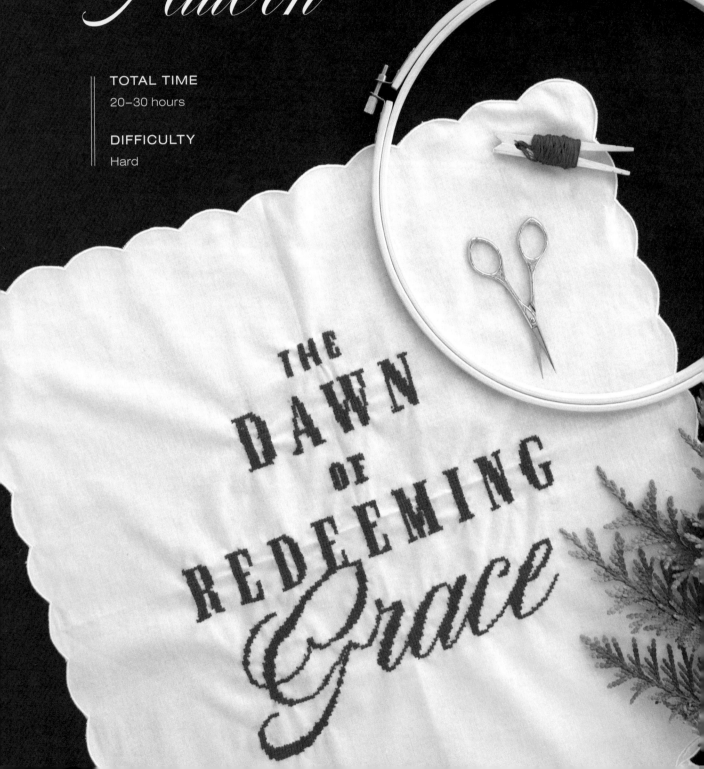

CROSS-STITCH
Pattern

THE
DAWN
OF
REDEEMING
Grace

In keeping with She Reads Truth's tradition, this year's Advent title comes from a lyric from a well-known Advent hymn. This year's title is from "Silent Night, Holy Night." As you work on this craft, use it as an opportunity to slow down, reflect on the advent of Christ, and rejoice in the dawn of redeeming grace. Once finished, display your cross-stitch as a visible reminder of this wondrous truth.

WHAT YOU NEED

 Cross-stitch pattern (Scan this QR code to view or download the cross-stitch pattern!)

14 count cross-stitch fabric (Or any fabric of your choice with a waste canvas on top)

11-inch embroidery hoop

Scissors

DMC embroidery floss in red (321)

Size 24 tapestry needle

WHAT TO DO: TO BEGIN

Find the center of the pattern (marked) and the center of your fabric. This is where you'll begin stitching. Center the fabric in the embroidery hoop and secure.

Cut a piece of embroidery floss the length of your arm, separate out 3 of the 6 threads, then thread them through your needle. Set the remaining 3 threads aside to use when you need to rethread.

To begin stitching, bring the threaded needle up through the back of the fabric, leaving a tail of about 1 inch of floss behind the fabric. Stitch the next 3 or 4 stitches over the tail. Clip off the extra thread.

WHAT TO DO: STITCHING

There are two methods. The first method is to work a row of half stitches ////, then work back \\\\ to complete the Xs. Use this method for most stitching. The second method is to complete each X as you go. Use this method for individual or complex rows of stitches.

The sign of a real cross-stitch pro is when all of the Xs are crossed in the same direction (that is, the top thread of the X always slants in the same direction, either \ or /). If you're a beginner, don't worry about this little detail. But if you're up for the challenge, give it a try!

WHAT TO DO: FINISHING

When you come to the end of a section of thread, use your needle to weave the thread through the last 5 or 6 stitches on the back side of your fabric. Clip the thread short so as not to leave a loose tail. When you begin a new section of thread, repeat the tail weaving method that you began with, and continue this cycle as you need more thread.

When your project is complete, remove it from the hoop. Before you display your work, smooth it out and remove wrinkles by placing another cloth on top of the needlework and pressing lightly with a warm iron. Display your finished creation in a frame or in the embroidery hoop you made it in!

HOPE AS OUR PERFECT

BUT THIS MAN,
AFTER OFFERING
ONE SACRIFICE FOR
SINS FOREVER, SAT
DOWN AT THE RIGHT
HAND OF GOD.

HEBREWS 10:12

Priest

Leviticus 9:1–7

THE PRIESTLY MINISTRY INAUGURATED

[1] On the eighth day Moses summoned Aaron, his sons, and the elders of Israel. [2] He said to Aaron, "Take a young bull for a sin offering and a ram for a burnt offering, both without blemish, and present them before the LORD. [3] And tell the Israelites: Take a male goat for a sin offering; a calf and a lamb, male yearlings without blemish, for a burnt offering; [4] an ox and a ram for a fellowship offering to sacrifice before the LORD; and a grain offering mixed with oil. For today the LORD is going to appear to you."

[5] They brought what Moses had commanded to the front of the tent of meeting, and the whole community came forward and stood before the LORD. [6] Moses said, "This is what the LORD commanded you to do, that the glory of the LORD may appear to you." [7] Then Moses said to Aaron, "Approach the altar and sacrifice your sin offering and your burnt offering; make atonement for yourself and the people. Sacrifice the people's offering and make atonement for them, as the LORD commanded."

Leviticus 16:29–34

[29] "This is to be a permanent statute for you: In the seventh month, on the tenth day of the month you are to practice self-denial and do no work, both the native and the alien who resides among you. [30] Atonement will be made for you on this day to cleanse you, and you will be clean from all your sins before the LORD. [31] It is a Sabbath of complete rest for you, and you must practice self-denial; it is a permanent statute. [32] The priest who is anointed and ordained to serve as high priest in place of his father will make atonement. He will put on the linen garments, the holy garments, [33] and make atonement for the most holy place. He will make atonement for the tent of meeting and the altar and will make atonement for the priests and all the people of the assembly. [34] This is to be a permanent statute for you, to make atonement for the Israelites once a year because of all their sins." And all this was done as the LORD commanded Moses.

Hebrews 4:14–16

OUR GREAT HIGH PRIEST

[14] Therefore, since we have a great high priest who has passed through the heavens—Jesus the Son of God—let us hold fast to our confession. [15] For we do not have a high priest who is unable to sympathize with our weaknesses, but one who has been tempted in every way as we are, yet without sin. [16] Therefore, let us approach the throne of grace with boldness, so that we may receive mercy and find grace to help us in time of need.

NOTES

Hebrews 5:1–10

CHRIST, A HIGH PRIEST

[1] For every high priest taken from among men is appointed in matters pertaining to God for the people, to offer both gifts and sacrifices for sins. [2] He is able to deal gently with those who are ignorant and are going astray, since he is also clothed with weakness. [3] Because of this, he must make an offering for his own sins as well as for the people. [4] No one takes this honor on himself; instead, a person is called by God, just as Aaron was. [5] In the same way, Christ did not exalt himself to become a high priest, but God who said to him,

> You are my Son;
> today I have become your Father,

[6] also says in another place,

> You are a priest forever
> according to the order of Melchizedek.

[7] During his earthly life, he offered prayers and appeals with loud cries and tears to the one who was able to save him from death, and he was heard because of his reverence. [8] Although he was the Son, he learned obedience from what he suffered. [9] After he was perfected, he became the source of eternal salvation for all who obey him, [10] and he was declared by God a high priest according to the order of Melchizedek.

Hebrews 10:10–14

[10] By this will, we have been sanctified through the offering of the body of Jesus Christ once for all time.

[11] Every priest stands day after day ministering and offering the same sacrifices time after time, which can never take away sins. [12] But this man, after offering one sacrifice for sins forever, sat down at the right hand of God. [13] He is now waiting until his enemies are made his footstool. [14] For by one offering he has perfected forever those who are sanctified.

RESPONSE

TIME   DATE

JESUS BRINGS HOPE AS OUR PERFECT PRIEST. WRITE A PRAYER
OF GRATITUDE, THANKING HIM FOR BEING OUR FAITHFUL HIGH PRIEST.

Hope

DAY
06

Hope FOR Healing

Isaiah 52:13–15

THE SERVANT'S SUFFERING AND EXALTATION

13 See, my servant will be successful;

he will be raised and lifted up and greatly exalted.

14 Just as many were appalled at you—

his appearance was so disfigured

that he did not look like a man,

and his form did not resemble a human being—

15 so he will sprinkle many nations.

Kings will shut their mouths because of him,

for they will see what had not been told them,

and they will understand what they had not heard.

Isaiah 53

1 Who has believed what we have heard?

And to whom has the arm of the LORD been revealed?

2 He grew up before him like a young plant

and like a root out of dry ground.

He didn't have an impressive form

or majesty that we should look at him,

no appearance that we should desire him.

3 He was despised and rejected by men,

a man of suffering who knew what sickness was.

He was like someone people turned away from;

he was despised, and we didn't value him.

4 Yet he himself bore our sicknesses, and he carried our pains;

but we in turn regarded him stricken,

struck down by God, and afflicted.

5 But he was pierced because of our rebellion,

crushed because of our iniquities;

punishment for our peace was on him,

and we are healed by his wounds.

6 We all went astray like sheep;

we all have turned to our own way;

and the LORD has punished him

for the iniquity of us all.

⁷ He was oppressed and afflicted,

yet he did not open his mouth.

Like a lamb led to the slaughter

and like a sheep silent before her shearers,

he did not open his mouth.

⁸ He was taken away because of oppression and judgment,

and who considered his fate?

For he was cut off from the land of the living;

he was struck because of my people's rebellion.

⁹ He was assigned a grave with the wicked,

but he was with a rich man at his death,

because he had done no violence

and had not spoken deceitfully.

¹⁰ Yet the Lᴏʀᴅ was pleased to crush him severely.

When you make him a guilt offering,

he will see his seed, he will prolong his days,

and by his hand, the Lᴏʀᴅ's pleasure will be accomplished.

¹¹ After his anguish,

he will see light and be satisfied.

By his knowledge,

my righteous servant will justify many,

and he will carry their iniquities.

¹² Therefore I will give him the many as a portion,

and he will receive the mighty as spoil,

because he willingly submitted to death,

and was counted among the rebels;

yet he bore the sin of many

and interceded for the rebels.

Matthew 15:29–30

HEALING MANY PEOPLE

²⁹ Moving on from there, Jesus passed along the Sea of Galilee. He went up on a mountain and sat there, ³⁰ and large crowds came to him, including the lame, the blind, the crippled, those unable to speak, and many others. They put them at his feet, and he healed them.

Mark 5:25–34

²⁵ Now a woman suffering from bleeding for twelve years ²⁶ had endured much under many doctors. She had spent everything she had and was not helped at all.

On the contrary, she became worse. [27] Having heard about Jesus, she came up behind him in the crowd and touched his clothing. [28] For she said, "If I just touch his clothes, I'll be made well." [29] Instantly her flow of blood ceased, and she sensed in her body that she was healed of her affliction.

[30] Immediately Jesus realized that power had gone out from him. He turned around in the crowd and said, "Who touched my clothes?"

[31] His disciples said to him, "You see the crowd pressing against you, and yet you say, 'Who touched me?'"

[32] But he was looking around to see who had done this. [33] The woman, with fear and trembling, knowing what had happened to her, came and fell down before him, and told him the whole truth. [34] "Daughter," he said to her, "your faith has saved you. Go in peace and be healed from your affliction."

Revelation 21:3–4

[3] Then I heard a loud voice from the throne: Look, God's dwelling is with humanity, and he will live with them. They will be his peoples, and God himself will be with them and will be their God. [4] He will wipe away every tear from their eyes. Death will be no more; grief, crying, and pain will be no more, because the previous things have passed away.

RESPONSE

TIME   DATE

JESUS BRINGS HOPE FOR HEALING. WRITE A PRAYER OF GRATITUDE,
THANKING HIM FOR BRINGING OUR ULTIMATE HEALING.

Hope

DAY 07

GRACE *Day*

TAKE THIS DAY TO CATCH UP ON
YOUR READING, PRAY, AND REST
IN THE PRESENCE OF THE LORD.

*F*OR GOD WHO SAID, "LET LIGHT SHINE OUT OF DARKNESS," HAS SHONE IN OUR HEARTS TO GIVE THE LIGHT OF THE KNOWLEDGE OF GOD'S GLORY IN THE FACE OF JESUS CHRIST.

2 CORINTHIANS 4:6

FOR A CHILD WILL BE BORN
FOR US, A SON WILL BE GIVEN
TO US, AND THE GOVERNMENT
WILL BE ON HIS SHOULDERS.
HE WILL BE NAMED
WONDERFUL COUNSELOR,
MIGHTY GOD, ETERNAL
FATHER, PRINCE OF PEACE.

Isaiah 9:6

THE
SECOND SUNDAY
OF
ADVENT:

The Hebrew word for peace, *shalom*, communicates a wholeness or completeness. Jesus came to a hurting world to bring it peace and to be a living example of shalom—defeating the enemy, reconciling people to Himself, and establishing a new kind of kingdom. In this week's readings, we will look at some of the specific ways that Jesus came to be our peace in our uncertain and chaotic world.

The title of each day of reading this week completes the statement "Jesus brings..."

PEACE THROUGH

His Sacrifice

Leviticus 4:32–35

³² "Or if the offering that he brings as a sin offering is a lamb, he is to bring an unblemished female. ³³ He is to lay his hand on the head of the sin offering and slaughter it as a sin offering at the place where the burnt offering is slaughtered. ³⁴ Then the priest is to take some of the blood of the sin offering with his finger and apply it to the horns of the altar of burnt offering. He is to pour out the rest of its blood at the base of the altar. ³⁵ He is to remove all its fat just as the fat of the lamb is removed from the fellowship sacrifice. The priest will burn it on the altar along with the food offerings to the LORD. In this way the priest will make atonement on his behalf for the sin he has committed, and he will be forgiven."

Leviticus 16:1–22

THE DAY OF ATONEMENT

¹ The LORD spoke to Moses after the death of two of Aaron's sons when they approached the presence of the LORD and died. ² The LORD said to Moses, "Tell your brother Aaron that he may not come whenever he wants into the holy place behind the curtain in front of the mercy seat on the ark or else he will die, because I appear in the cloud above the mercy seat.

³ "Aaron is to enter the most holy place in this way: with a young bull for a sin offering and a ram for a burnt offering. ⁴ He is to wear a holy linen tunic, and linen undergarments are to be on his body. He is to tie a linen sash around him and wrap his head with a linen turban. These are holy garments; he must bathe his body with water before he wears them. ⁵ He is to take from the Israelite community two male goats for a sin offering and one ram for a burnt offering.

⁶ "Aaron will present the bull for his sin offering and make atonement for himself and his household. ⁷ Next he will take the two goats and place them before the LORD at the entrance to the tent of meeting. ⁸ After Aaron casts lots for the two goats, one lot for the LORD and the other for an uninhabitable place, ⁹ he is to present the goat chosen by lot for the LORD and sacrifice it as a sin offering. ¹⁰ But the goat chosen by lot for an uninhabitable place is to be presented alive before the LORD to make atonement with it by sending it into the wilderness for an uninhabitable place.

¹¹ "When Aaron presents the bull for his sin offering and makes atonement for himself and his household, he will slaughter the bull for his sin offering. ¹² Then he is to take

a firepan full of blazing coals from the altar before the LORD and two handfuls of finely ground fragrant incense, and bring them inside the curtain. ¹³ He is to put the incense on the fire before the LORD, so that the cloud of incense covers the mercy seat that is over the testimony, or else he will die. ¹⁴ He is to take some of the bull's blood and sprinkle it with his finger against the east side of the mercy seat; then he will sprinkle some of the blood with his finger before the mercy seat seven times.

¹⁵ "When he slaughters the male goat for the people's sin offering and brings its blood inside the curtain, he will do the same with its blood as he did with the bull's blood: He is to sprinkle it against the mercy seat and in front of it. ¹⁶ He will make atonement for the most holy place in this way for all their sins because of the Israelites' impurities and rebellious acts. He will do the same for the tent of meeting that remains among them, because it is surrounded by their impurities. ¹⁷ No one may be in the tent of meeting from the time he enters to make atonement in the most holy place until he leaves after he has made atonement for himself, his household, and the whole assembly of Israel. ¹⁸ Then he will go out to the altar that is before the LORD and make atonement for it. He is to take some of the bull's blood and some of the goat's blood and put it on the horns on all sides of the altar. ¹⁹ He is to sprinkle some of the blood on it with his finger seven times to cleanse and set it apart from the Israelites' impurities.

²⁰ "When he has finished making atonement for the most holy place, the tent of meeting, and the altar, he is to present the live male goat. ²¹ Aaron will lay both his hands on the head of the live goat and confess over it all the Israelites' iniquities and rebellious acts—all their sins. He is to put them on the goat's head and send it away into the wilderness by the man appointed for the task. ²² The goat will carry all their iniquities into a desolate land, and the man will release it there."

John 1:29

The next day John saw Jesus coming toward him and said, "Look, the Lamb of God, who takes away the sin of the world!"

Hebrews 10:1–10

THE PERFECT SACRIFICE

¹ Since the law has only a shadow of the good things to come, and not the reality itself of those things, it can never perfect the worshipers by the same sacrifices they continually offer year after year. ² Otherwise, wouldn't they have stopped being offered, since the worshipers, purified once and for all, would no longer have any consciousness of sins? ³ But in the sacrifices there is a reminder of sins year after year. ⁴ For it is impossible for the blood of bulls and goats to take away sins.

NOTES

⁵ Therefore, as he was coming into the world, he said:

> You did not desire sacrifice and offering,
> but you prepared a body for me.
> ⁶ You did not delight
> in whole burnt offerings and sin offerings.
> ⁷ Then I said, "See—
> it is written about me
> in the scroll—
> I have come to do your will, God."

⁸ After he says above, You did not desire or delight in sacrifices and offerings, whole burnt offerings and sin offerings (which are offered according to the law), ⁹ he then says, See, I have come to do your will. He takes away the first to establish the second.

¹⁰ By this will, we have been sanctified through the offering of the body of Jesus Christ once for all time.

2 Corinthians 5:21

He made the one who did not know sin to be sin for us, so that in him we might become the righteousness of God.

1 Peter 1:17–21

¹⁷ If you appeal to the Father who judges impartially according to each one's work, you are to conduct yourselves in reverence during your time living as strangers. ¹⁸ For you know that you were redeemed from your empty way of life inherited from your ancestors, not with perishable things like silver or gold, ¹⁹ but with the precious blood of Christ, like that of an unblemished and spotless lamb. ²⁰ He was foreknown before the foundation of the world but was revealed in these last times for you. ²¹ Through him you believe in God, who raised him from the dead and gave him glory, so that your faith and hope are in God.

RESPONSE

TIME DATE

As you respond this week, consider praying about how each day's reading leads you to praise, shapes your perspective on what it means to experience peace, and equips you to encourage those in your community.

JESUS BRINGS PEACE THROUGH HIS SACRIFICE. WRITE A PRAYER OF GRATITUDE, THANKING HIM FOR BEING THE SPOTLESS LAMB OF GOD.

Peace

CANDIED *Bacon*

INGREDIENTS

1½ pounds bacon

½ cup brown sugar

Pepper

DIRECTIONS

Preheat oven to 375°F. Line two baking sheets with aluminum foil, and place an oven-safe wire rack on top of each pan. Line bacon slices on wire racks (perpendicular so the pieces don't fall through). Sprinkle brown sugar on bacon, spreading evenly over each slice. Season with pepper.

Bake for 18 to 22 minutes, or until brown sugar is melted and bacon has reached the desired crispiness.

Remove from oven, and let cool on the wire racks for 5 minutes before serving.

PREP TIME	COOK TIME	YIELD
5 minutes	18–22 minutes	8–10 servings

Peace

THROUGH

Reconciliation

Jeremiah 31:10–11, 31–34

[10] Nations, hear the word of the Lord,
and tell it among the far off coasts and islands!
Say, "The one who scattered Israel will gather him.
He will watch over him as a shepherd guards his flock,
[11] for the Lord has ransomed Jacob
and redeemed him from the power of one stronger than he."

…

THE NEW COVENANT

[31] "Look, the days are coming"—this is the Lord's declaration—"when I will make a new covenant with the house of Israel and with the house of Judah. [32] This one will not be like the covenant I made with their ancestors on the day I took them by the hand to lead them out of the land of Egypt—my covenant that they broke even though I am their master"—the Lord's declaration. [33] "Instead, this is the covenant I will make with the house of Israel after those days"—the Lord's declaration. "I will put my teaching within them and write it on their hearts. I will be their God, and they will be my people. [34] No longer will one teach his neighbor or his brother, saying, 'Know the Lord,' for they will all know me, from the least to the greatest of them"—this is the Lord's declaration. "For I will forgive their iniquity and never again remember their sin."

Ephesians 2

FROM DEATH TO LIFE

[1] And you were dead in your trespasses and sins [2] in which you previously walked according to the ways of this world, according to the ruler of the power of the air, the spirit now working in the disobedient. [3] We too all previously lived among them in our fleshly desires, carrying out the inclinations of our flesh and thoughts, and we were by nature children under wrath as the others were also. [4] But God, who is rich in mercy, because of his great love that he had for us, [5] made us alive with Christ even though we were dead in trespasses. You are saved by grace! [6] He also raised us up with him and seated us with him in the heavens in Christ Jesus, [7] so that in the coming ages he might display the immeasurable riches of his grace through his kindness to us in Christ Jesus. [8] For you are saved by grace through faith, and this is not from yourselves; it is God's gift— [9] not from works, so that no one can boast. [10] For we are his workmanship, created in Christ Jesus for good works, which God prepared ahead of time for us to do.

UNITY IN CHRIST

[11] So, then, remember that at one time you were Gentiles in the flesh—called "the uncircumcised" by those called "the circumcised," which is done in the flesh by human hands. [12] At that time you were without Christ, excluded from the citizenship of Israel, and foreigners to the covenants of promise, without hope and without God in the world. [13] But now in Christ Jesus, you who were far away have been brought near by the blood of Christ.

[14] For he is our peace, who made both groups one and tore down the dividing wall of hostility.

In his flesh, [15] he made of no effect the law consisting of commands and expressed in regulations, so that he might create in himself one new man from the two, resulting in peace. [16] He did this so that he might reconcile both to God in one body through the cross by which he put the hostility to death. [17] He came and proclaimed the good news of peace to you who were far away and peace to those who were near. [18] For through him we both have access in one Spirit to the Father. [19] So, then, you are no longer foreigners and strangers, but fellow citizens with the saints, and members of God's household, [20] built on the foundation of the apostles and prophets, with Christ Jesus himself as the cornerstone. [21] In him the whole building, being put together, grows into a holy temple in the Lord. [22] In him you are also being built together for God's dwelling in the Spirit.

Romans 5:6–11

THE JUSTIFIED ARE RECONCILED

[6] For while we were still helpless, at the right time, Christ died for the ungodly. [7] For rarely will someone die for a just person—though for a good person perhaps someone might even dare to die. [8] But God proves his own love for us in that

while we were still sinners, Christ died for us. [9] How much more then, since we have now been justified by his blood, will we be saved through him from wrath. [10] For if, while we were enemies, we were reconciled to God through the death of his Son, then how much more, having been reconciled, will we be saved by his life. [11] And not only that, but we also boast in God through our Lord Jesus Christ, through whom we have now received this reconciliation.

Colossians 1:21–23

[21] Once you were alienated and hostile in your minds as expressed in your evil actions. [22] But now he has reconciled you by his physical body through his death, to present you holy, faultless, and blameless before him— [23] if indeed you remain grounded and steadfast in the faith and are not shifted away from the hope of the gospel that you heard. This gospel has been proclaimed in all creation under heaven, and I, Paul, have become a servant of it.

RESPONSE

TIME   DATE

JESUS BRINGS PEACE THROUGH RECONCILIATION. WRITE A PRAYER
OF GRATITUDE, THANKING HIM FOR RECONCILING US TO GOD AND
TO ONE ANOTHER.

Peace

Peace THROUGH
FULFILLMENT

"Don't think that I came to abolish the Law or the Prophets.
I did not come to abolish but to fulfill."

Matthew 5:17

Exodus 20:1–17

¹ Then God spoke all these words:

² I am the LORD your God, who brought you out of the land of Egypt, out of the place of slavery.

³ Do not have other gods besides me.

⁴ Do not make an idol for yourself, whether in the shape of anything in the heavens above or on the earth below or in the waters under the earth. ⁵ Do not bow in worship to them, and do not serve them; for I, the LORD your God, am a jealous God, bringing the consequences of the fathers' iniquity on the children to the third and fourth generations of those who hate me, ⁶ but showing faithful love to a thousand generations of those who love me and keep my commands.

⁷ Do not misuse the name of the LORD your God, because the LORD will not leave anyone unpunished who misuses his name.

⁸ Remember the Sabbath day, to keep it holy: ⁹ You are to labor six days and do all your work, ¹⁰ but the seventh day is a Sabbath to the LORD your God. You must not do any work—you, your son or daughter, your male or female servant, your livestock, or the resident alien who is within your city gates. ¹¹ For the LORD made the heavens and the earth, the sea, and everything in them in six days; then he rested on the seventh day. Therefore the LORD blessed the Sabbath day and declared it holy.

¹² Honor your father and your mother so that you may have a long life in the land that the LORD your God is giving you.

¹³ Do not murder.

¹⁴ Do not commit adultery.

¹⁵ Do not steal.

¹⁶ Do not give false testimony against your neighbor.

¹⁷ Do not covet your neighbor's house. Do not covet your neighbor's wife, his male or female servant, his ox or donkey, or anything that belongs to your neighbor.

Matthew 5:17–48

CHRIST FULFILLS THE LAW

¹⁷ "Don't think that I came to abolish the Law or the Prophets. I did not come to abolish but to fulfill. ¹⁸ For truly I tell you, until heaven and earth pass away, not the smallest letter or one stroke of a letter will pass away from the law until all things are accomplished. ¹⁹ Therefore, whoever breaks one of the least of these commands and teaches others to do the same will be called least in the kingdom of heaven. But whoever does and teaches these commands will be called great in the kingdom of heaven. ²⁰ For I tell you, unless your righteousness surpasses that of the scribes and Pharisees, you will never get into the kingdom of heaven.

MURDER BEGINS IN THE HEART

²¹ "You have heard that it was said to our ancestors, Do not murder, and whoever murders will be subject to judgment. ²² But I tell you, everyone who is angry with his brother or sister will be subject to judgment. Whoever insults his brother or sister will be subject to the court. Whoever says, 'You fool!' will be subject to hellfire. ²³ So if you are offering your gift on the altar, and there you remember that your brother or sister has something against you, ²⁴ leave your gift there in front of the altar. First go and be reconciled with your brother or sister, and then come and offer your gift. ²⁵ Reach a settlement quickly with your adversary while you're on the way with him to the court, or your adversary will hand you over to the judge, and the judge to the officer, and you will be thrown into prison. ²⁶ Truly I tell you, you will never get out of there until you have paid the last penny.

ADULTERY BEGINS IN THE HEART

²⁷ "You have heard that it was said, Do not commit adultery. ²⁸ But I tell you, everyone who looks at a woman lustfully has already committed adultery with her in his heart. ²⁹ If your right eye causes you to sin, gouge it out and throw it away. For it is better that you lose one of the parts of your body than for your whole body to be thrown into hell. ³⁰ And if your right hand causes you to sin, cut it off and throw it away. For it is better that you lose one of the parts of your body than for your whole body to go into hell.

DIVORCE PRACTICES CENSURED

³¹ "It was also said, Whoever divorces his wife must give her a written notice of divorce. ³² But I tell you, everyone who divorces his wife, except in a case of sexual

immorality, causes her to commit adultery. And whoever marries a divorced woman commits adultery.

TELL THE TRUTH

[33] "Again, you have heard that it was said to our ancestors, You must not break your oath, but you must keep your oaths to the Lord. [34] But I tell you, don't take an oath at all: either by heaven, because it is God's throne; [35] or by the earth, because it is his footstool; or by Jerusalem, because it is the city of the great King. [36] Do not swear by your head, because you cannot make a single hair white or black. [37] But let your 'yes' mean 'yes,' and your 'no' mean 'no.' Anything more than this is from the evil one.

GO THE SECOND MILE

[38] "You have heard that it was said, An eye for an eye and a tooth for a tooth. [39] But I tell you, don't resist an evildoer. On the contrary, if anyone slaps you on your right cheek, turn the other to him also. [40] As for the one who wants to sue you and take away your shirt, let him have your coat as well. [41] And if anyone forces you to go one mile, go with him two. [42] Give to the one who asks you, and don't turn away from the one who wants to borrow from you.

LOVE YOUR ENEMIES

[43] "You have heard that it was said, Love your neighbor and hate your enemy. [44] But I tell you, love your enemies and pray for those who persecute you, [45] so that you may be children of your Father in heaven. For he causes his sun to rise on the evil and the good, and sends rain on the righteous and the unrighteous. [46] For if you love those who love you, what reward will you have? Don't even the tax collectors do the same? [47] And if you greet only your brothers and sisters, what are you doing out of the ordinary? Don't even the Gentiles do the same? [48] Be perfect, therefore, as your heavenly Father is perfect."

Romans 8:1-4

THE LIFE-GIVING SPIRIT

[1] Therefore, there is now no condemnation for those in Christ Jesus, [2] because the law of the Spirit of life in Christ Jesus has set you free from the law of sin and death.

[3] **For what the law could not do since it was weakened by the flesh, God did.**

He condemned sin in the flesh by sending his own Son in the likeness of sinful flesh as a sin offering, [4] in order that the law's requirement would be fulfilled in us who do not walk according to the flesh but according to the Spirit.

RESPONSE

TIME   DATE

JESUS BRINGS PEACE THROUGH FULFILLMENT. WRITE A PRAYER OF
GRATITUDE, THANKING HIM FOR PERFECTLY FULFILLING THE LAW.

Peace

Peace IN HIS ETERNAL Reign

Isaiah 9:1–7

BIRTH OF THE PRINCE OF PEACE

[1] Nevertheless, the gloom of the distressed land will not be like that of the former times when he humbled the land of Zebulun and the land of Naphtali. But in the future he will bring honor to the way of the sea, to the land east of the Jordan, and to Galilee of the nations.

[2] The people walking in darkness
have seen a great light;
a light has dawned
on those living in the land of darkness.
[3] You have enlarged the nation
and increased its joy.
The people have rejoiced before you
as they rejoice at harvest time
and as they rejoice when dividing spoils.
[4] For you have shattered their oppressive yoke
and the rod on their shoulders,
the staff of their oppressor,
just as you did on the day of Midian.
[5] For every trampling boot of battle
and the bloodied garments of war
will be burned as fuel for the fire.
[6] For a child will be born for us,
a son will be given to us,
and the government will be on his shoulders.
He will be named
Wonderful Counselor, Mighty God,
Eternal Father, Prince of Peace.
[7] The dominion will be vast,
and its prosperity will never end.
He will reign on the throne of David

and over his kingdom,
to establish and sustain it
with justice and righteousness from now on and forever.
The zeal of the LORD of Armies will accomplish this.

2 Samuel 7:8–16

[8] "So now this is what you are to say to my servant David: 'This is what the LORD of Armies says: I took you from the pasture, from tending the flock, to be ruler over my people Israel. [9] I have been with you wherever you have gone, and I have destroyed all your enemies before you. I will make a great name for you like that of the greatest on the earth. [10] I will designate a place for my people Israel and plant them, so that they may live there and not be disturbed again. Evildoers will not continue to oppress them as they have done [11] ever since the day I ordered judges to be over my people Israel. I will give you rest from all your enemies.'

"'The LORD declares to you: The LORD himself will make a house for you. [12] When your time comes and you rest with your ancestors, I will raise up after you your descendant, who will come from your body, and I will establish his kingdom. [13] He is the one who will build a house for my name, and I will establish the throne of his kingdom forever. [14] I will be his father, and he will be my son. When he does wrong, I will discipline him with a rod of men and blows from mortals. [15] But my faithful love will never leave him as it did when I removed it from Saul, whom I removed from before you. [16] Your house and kingdom will endure before me forever, and your throne will be established forever.'"

Isaiah 11:1–6

REIGN OF THE DAVIDIC KING

[1] Then a shoot will grow from the stump of Jesse,
and a branch from his roots will bear fruit.
[2] The Spirit of the LORD will rest on him—
a Spirit of wisdom and understanding,
a Spirit of counsel and strength,
a Spirit of knowledge and of the fear of the LORD.
[3] His delight will be in the fear of the LORD.
He will not judge
by what he sees with his eyes,
he will not execute justice
by what he hears with his ears,
[4] but he will judge the poor righteously
and execute justice for the oppressed of the land.
He will strike the land
with a scepter from his mouth,
and he will kill the wicked
with a command from his lips.
[5] Righteousness will be a belt around his hips;
faithfulness will be a belt around his waist.

[6] The wolf will dwell with the lamb,
and the leopard will lie down with the goat.
The calf, the young lion, and the fattened calf
   will be together,
and a child will lead them.

Luke 1:32–33

[32] He will be great and will be called the Son of the Most High, and the Lord God will give him the throne of his father David. [33] He will reign over the house of Jacob forever, and his kingdom will have no end.

Matthew 22:41–46

THE QUESTION ABOUT THE MESSIAH

[41] While the Pharisees were together, Jesus questioned them, [42] "What do you think about the Messiah? Whose son is he?"

They replied, "David's."

[43] He asked them, "How is it then that David, inspired by the Spirit, calls him 'Lord':

   [44] The Lord declared to my Lord,
   'Sit at my right hand
   until I put your enemies under your feet'?

[45] "If David calls him 'Lord,' how, then, can he be his son?" [46] No one was able to answer him at all, and from that day no one dared to question him anymore.

Acts 2:29–36

29 Brothers and sisters, I can confidently speak to you about the patriarch David: He is both dead and buried, and his tomb is with us to this day. 30 Since he was a prophet, he knew that God had sworn an oath to him to seat one of his descendants on his throne. 31 Seeing what was to come, he spoke concerning the resurrection of the Messiah: He was not abandoned in Hades, and his flesh did not experience decay.

32 God has raised this Jesus; we are all witnesses of this. 33 Therefore, since he has been exalted to the right hand of God and has received from the Father the promised Holy Spirit, he has poured out what you both see and hear. 34 For it was not David who ascended into the heavens, but he himself says:

The Lord declared to my Lord,
"Sit at my right hand
35 until I make your enemies your footstool."

36 Therefore let all the house of Israel know with certainty that God has made this Jesus, whom you crucified, both Lord and Messiah.

RESPONSE

TIME   DATE

JESUS BRINGS PEACE IN HIS ETERNAL REIGN. WRITE A PRAYER OF
GRATITUDE, THANKING HIM FOR RULING AND REIGNING AS OUR ONE
TRUE KING.

Peace

Angels
WE HAVE HEARD
ON HIGH

WORDS

Traditional French carol

MUSIC

Traditional French melody

1. An - gels we have heard on high, Sweet-ly sing - ing o'er the plains;
2. Shep - herds, why this ju - bi - lee? Why your joy - ous strains pro - long?
3. Come to Beth - le - hem, and see Him whose birth the an - gels sing;
4. See with - in a man - ger laid Je - sus, Lord of heav'n and earth!

And the moun - tains in re - ply, Ech - o back their joy - ous strains.
Say what may the tid - ings be Which in - spire your heav'n - ly song?
Come, a - dore on bend - ed knee Christ the Lord, the new - born King.
Ma - ry, Jo - seph, lend your aid, With us sing our Sav - ior's birth.

Chorus

Glo - - - ri - a in ex-cel-sis De-o!

Glo - - - ri - a in ex-cel-sisDe - o!

PEACE BY DEFEATING

THE SON OF GOD
WAS REVEALED
FOR THIS PURPOSE:
TO DESTROY THE
DEVIL'S WORKS.

1 JOHN 3:8

Death

Genesis 3:15

I will put hostility between you and the woman,
and between your offspring and her offspring.
He will strike your head,
and you will strike his heel.

Mark 3:22–27

²² The scribes who had come down from Jerusalem said, "He is possessed by Beelzebul," and, "He drives out demons by the ruler of the demons."

²³ So he summoned them and spoke to them in parables: "How can Satan drive out Satan? ²⁴ If a kingdom is divided against itself, that kingdom cannot stand. ²⁵ If a house is divided against itself, that house cannot stand. ²⁶ And if Satan opposes himself and is divided, he cannot stand but is finished. ²⁷ But no one can enter a strong man's house and plunder his possessions unless he first ties up the strong man. Then he can plunder his house."

Hebrews 2:5–18
JESUS AND HUMANITY

⁵ For he has not subjected to angels the world to come that we are talking about. ⁶ But someone somewhere has testified:

What is man that you remember him,
or the son of man that you care for him?
⁷ You made him lower than the angels
for a short time;
you crowned him with glory and honor
⁸ and subjected everything under his feet.

For in subjecting everything to him, he left nothing that is not subject to him. As it is, we do not yet see everything subjected to him. ⁹ But we do see Jesus—made lower than the angels for a short time so that by God's grace he might taste death for everyone—crowned with glory and honor because he suffered death.

¹⁰ For in bringing many sons and daughters to glory, it was entirely appropriate that God—for whom and through whom all things exist—should make the pioneer of their salvation perfect through sufferings. ¹¹ For the one who sanctifies and those who are sanctified all have one Father. That is why Jesus is not ashamed to call them brothers and sisters, ¹² saying:

I will proclaim your name to my brothers and sisters;
I will sing hymns to you in the congregation.

¹³ Again, I will trust in him. And again, Here I am with the children God gave me.

¹⁴ Now since the children have flesh and blood in common, Jesus also shared in these, so that through his death he might destroy the one holding the power of death—that is, the devil— ¹⁵ and free those who were held in slavery all their lives by the fear of death. ¹⁶ For it is clear that he does not reach out to help angels, but to help Abraham's offspring. ¹⁷ Therefore, he had to be like his brothers and sisters in every way, so that he could become a merciful and faithful high priest in matters pertaining to God, to make atonement for the sins of the people. ¹⁸ For since he himself has suffered when he was tempted, he is able to help those who are tempted.

1 Corinthians 15:24–26

²⁴ Then comes the end, when he hands over the kingdom to God the Father, when he abolishes all rule and all authority and power. ²⁵ For he must reign until he puts all his enemies under his feet. ²⁶ The last enemy to be abolished is death.

1 John 3:7–8

⁷ Little children, let no one deceive you. The one who does what is right is righteous, just as he is righteous. ⁸ The one who commits sin is of the devil, for the devil has sinned

from the beginning. The Son of God was revealed for this purpose: to destroy the devil's works.

Revelation 12:10–12

[10] Then I heard a loud voice in heaven say,

The salvation and the power
and the kingdom of our God
and the authority of his Christ
have now come,
because the accuser of our brothers and sisters,
who accuses them
before our God day and night,
has been thrown down.
[11] They conquered him
by the blood of the Lamb
and by the word of their testimony;
for they did not love their lives
to the point of death.
[12] Therefore rejoice, you heavens,
and you who dwell in them!
Woe to the earth and the sea,
because the devil has come down to you
with great fury,
because he knows his time is short.

RESPONSE

TIME   DATE

JESUS BRINGS PEACE BY DEFEATING DEATH. WRITE A PRAYER
OF GRATITUDE, THANKING HIM FOR DEFEATING DEATH FOREVER.

Peace

DAY 14

GRACE *Day*

TAKE THIS DAY TO CATCH UP ON
YOUR READING, PRAY, AND REST
IN THE PRESENCE OF THE LORD.

E CAME AND PROCLAIMED
THE GOOD NEWS OF PEACE TO
YOU WHO WERE FAR AWAY AND
PEACE TO THOSE WHO WERE NEAR.

EPHESIANS 2:17

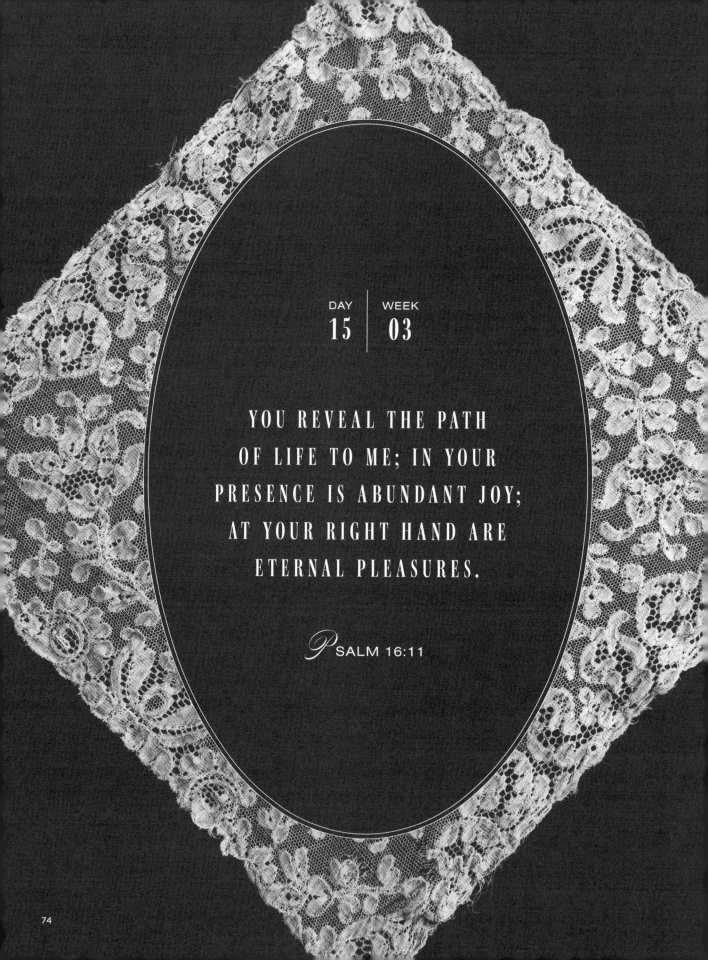

DAY | WEEK
15 | **03**

YOU REVEAL THE PATH
OF LIFE TO ME; IN YOUR
PRESENCE IS ABUNDANT JOY;
AT YOUR RIGHT HAND ARE
ETERNAL PLEASURES.

*P*SALM 16:11

THE
THIRD SUNDAY
OF
ADVENT:

Joy is in the celebration of all the ways God
redeemed and restored His people in the sending
of His Son into the world. During Advent, we
remember and praise God for freely giving us joy
through the work of Christ, and we receive His joy
in remembering all Jesus has done to bring us
back to God. In this week's readings, we will look at
some of the specific ways that Jesus came to bring
us joy through His life, death, and resurrection.

The title of each day of reading this week completes the
statement "Jesus brings..."

Joy THROUGH **Salvation**

Isaiah 49:8–13

⁸ This is what the LORD says:

> I will answer you in a time of favor,
> and I will help you in the day of salvation.
> I will keep you, and I will appoint you
> to be a covenant for the people,
> to restore the land,
> to make them possess the desolate inheritances,
> ⁹ saying to the prisoners, "Come out,"
> and to those who are in darkness, "Show yourselves."
> They will feed along the pathways,
> and their pastures will be on all the barren heights.
> ¹⁰ They will not hunger or thirst,
> the scorching heat or sun will not strike them;
> for their compassionate one will guide them,
> and lead them to springs.
> ¹¹ I will make all my mountains into a road,
> and my highways will be raised up.
> ¹² See, these will come from far away,
> from the north and from the west,
> and from the land of Sinim.
>
> ¹³ Shout for joy, you heavens!
> Earth, rejoice!
> Mountains break into joyful shouts!
> For the LORD has comforted his people,
> and will have compassion on his afflicted ones.

Matthew 9:9–13

THE CALL OF MATTHEW

⁹ As Jesus went on from there, he saw a man named Matthew sitting at the tax office, and he said to him, "Follow me," and he got up and followed him.

¹⁰ While he was reclining at the table in the house, many tax collectors and sinners came to eat with Jesus and his disciples. ¹¹ When the Pharisees saw this, they asked his disciples, "Why does your teacher eat with tax collectors and sinners?"

¹² Now when he heard this, he said, "It is not those who are well who need a doctor, but those who are sick. ¹³ Go and learn what this means: I desire mercy and not sacrifice. For I didn't come to call the righteous, but sinners."

Luke 4:16–30

REJECTION AT NAZARETH

[16] He came to Nazareth, where he had been brought up. As usual, he entered the synagogue on the Sabbath day and stood up to read. [17] The scroll of the prophet Isaiah was given to him, and unrolling the scroll, he found the place where it was written:

> [18] The Spirit of the Lord is on me,
> because he has anointed me
> to preach good news to the poor.
> He has sent me
> to proclaim release to the captives
> and recovery of sight to the blind,
> to set free the oppressed,
> [19] to proclaim the year of the Lord's favor.

[20] He then rolled up the scroll, gave it back to the attendant, and sat down. And the eyes of everyone in the synagogue were fixed on him. [21] He began by saying to them, "Today as you listen, this Scripture has been fulfilled."

[22] They were all speaking well of him and were amazed by the gracious words that came from his mouth; yet they said, "Isn't this Joseph's son?"

[23] Then he said to them, "No doubt you will quote this proverb to me: 'Doctor, heal yourself. What we've heard that took place in Capernaum, do here in your hometown also.'"

[24] He also said, "Truly I tell you, no prophet is accepted in his hometown. [25] But I say to you, there were certainly many widows in Israel in Elijah's days, when the sky was shut up for three years and six months while a great famine came over all the land. [26] Yet Elijah was not sent to any of them except a widow at Zarephath in Sidon. [27] And in the prophet Elisha's time, there were many in Israel who had leprosy, and yet not one of them was cleansed except Naaman the Syrian."

[28] When they heard this, everyone in the synagogue was enraged. [29] They got up, drove him out of town, and brought him to the edge of the hill that their town was built on, intending to hurl him over the cliff. [30] But he passed right through the crowd and went on his way.

Luke 19:1–10

JESUS VISITS ZACCHAEUS

[1] He entered Jericho and was passing through. [2] There was a man named Zacchaeus who was a chief tax collector, and he was rich. [3] He was trying to see who Jesus was,

but he was not able because of the crowd, since he was a short man. [4] So running ahead, he climbed up a sycamore tree to see Jesus, since he was about to pass that way. [5] When Jesus came to the place, he looked up and said to him, "Zacchaeus, hurry and come down because today it is necessary for me to stay at your house."

[6] So he quickly came down and welcomed him joyfully. [7] All who saw it began to complain, "He's gone to stay with a sinful man."

[8] But Zacchaeus stood there and said to the Lord, "Look, I'll give half of my possessions to the poor, Lord. And if I have extorted anything from anyone, I'll pay back four times as much."

[9] "Today salvation has come to this house," Jesus told him, "because he too is a son of Abraham. [10] For the Son of Man has come to seek and to save the lost."

1 John 4:14

And we have seen and we testify that the Father has sent his Son as the world's Savior.

RESPONSE

TIME   DATE

As you respond this week, consider praying about how each day's reading leads you to praise, shapes your perspective on what it means to experience joy, and equips you to encourage those in your community.

JESUS BRINGS JOY THROUGH SALVATION. WRITE A PRAYER OF GRATITUDE,
THANKING HIM FOR COMING TO SEEK AND SAVE THE LOST.

Joy

TAPER
Candles

Throughout this reading plan, we've been exploring the Advent themes that correspond with the traditional Advent candles. Here's a festive way to use candles to decorate your Christmas morning breakfast table or make your own Advent wreath. Consider using the traditional Advent colors (see page 15!), or you can use a neutral color palette like we did here. As you pass by your candles throughout this season, let them serve as a reminder of the hope, peace, joy, and love we have in Christ.

TOTAL TIME	DIFFICULTY
15 minutes	Easy

WHAT YOU NEED

Clear bottles
Greenery
Taper candles

WHAT TO DO

Select a bottle with an opening the size of your candle, and place your desired amount of greenery in it. Place a taper candle in the opening of the bottle. Repeat this process with whatever assortment of bottles and candles you would like.

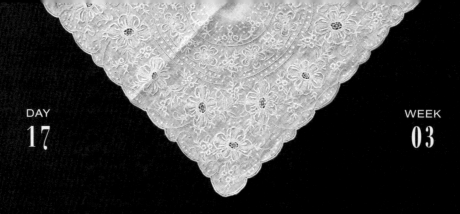

JOY THROUGH

Redemption

Isaiah 43:1–7

RESTORATION OF ISRAEL

[1] Now this is what the LORD says—
the one who created you, Jacob,
and the one who formed you, Israel—
"Do not fear, for I have redeemed you;
I have called you by your name; you are mine.
[2] When you pass through the waters,
I will be with you,
and the rivers will not overwhelm you.
When you walk through the fire,
you will not be scorched,
and the flame will not burn you.
[3] For I am the LORD your God,
the Holy One of Israel, and your Savior.
I have given Egypt as a ransom for you,
Cush and Seba in your place.
[4] Because you are precious in my sight
and honored, and I love you,
I will give people in exchange for you
and nations instead of your life.
[5] Do not fear, for I am with you;
I will bring your descendants from the east,
and gather you from the west.
[6] I will say to the north, 'Give them up!'
and to the south, 'Do not hold them back!'
Bring my sons from far away,
and my daughters from the ends of the earth—
[7] everyone who bears my name
and is created for my glory.
I have formed them; indeed, I have made them."

Psalm 111

PRAISE FOR THE LORD'S WORKS

[1] Hallelujah!
I will praise the LORD with all my heart
in the assembly of the upright and in the congregation.
[2] The LORD's works are great,
studied by all who delight in them.
[3] All that he does is splendid and majestic;
his righteousness endures forever.
[4] He has caused his wondrous works to be remembered.
The LORD is gracious and compassionate.

He has provided food for those who fear him;

he remembers his covenant forever.

[6] He has shown his people the power of his works

by giving them the inheritance of the nations.

[7] The works of his hands are truth and justice;

all his instructions are trustworthy.

[8] They are established forever and ever,

enacted in truth and in uprightness.

[9] He has sent redemption to his people.

He has ordained his covenant forever.

His name is holy and awe-inspiring.

[10] The fear of the LORD is the beginning of wisdom;

all who follow his instructions have good insight.

His praise endures forever.

Luke 15:11–32

THE PARABLE OF THE LOST SON

[11] He also said, "A man had two sons. [12] The younger of them said to his father, 'Father, give me the share of the estate I have coming to me.' So he distributed the assets to them. [13] Not many days later, the younger son gathered together all he had and traveled to a distant country, where he squandered his estate in foolish living. [14] After he had spent everything, a severe famine struck that country, and he had nothing. [15] Then he went to work for one of the citizens of that country, who sent him into his fields to feed pigs. [16] He longed to eat his fill from the pods that the pigs were eating, but no one would give him anything. [17] When he came to his senses, he said, 'How many of my father's hired workers have more than enough food, and here I am dying of hunger! [18] I'll get up, go to my father, and say to him, "Father, I have sinned against heaven and in your sight. [19] I'm no longer worthy to be called your son. Make me like one of your hired workers."' [20] So he got up and went to his father. But while the son was still a long way off, his father saw him and was filled with compassion. He ran, threw his arms around his neck, and kissed him. [21] The son said to him, 'Father, I have sinned against heaven and in your sight. I'm no longer worthy to be called your son.'

[22] "But the father told his servants, 'Quick! Bring out the best robe and put it on him; put a ring on his finger and sandals on his feet. [23] Then bring the fattened calf and slaughter it, and let's celebrate with a feast, [24] because this son of mine was dead and is alive again; he was lost and is found!' So they began to celebrate.

[25] "Now his older son was in the field; as he came near the house, he heard music and dancing. [26] So he summoned one of the servants, questioning what these things

DAY 17   83

meant. [27] 'Your brother is here,' he told him, 'and your father has slaughtered the fattened calf because he has him back safe and sound.'

[28] "Then he became angry and didn't want to go in. So his father came out and pleaded with him. [29] But he replied to his father, 'Look, I have been slaving many years for you, and I have never disobeyed your orders, yet you never gave me a goat so that I could celebrate with my friends. [30] But when this son of yours came, who has devoured your assets with prostitutes, you slaughtered the fattened calf for him.'

[31] "'Son,' he said to him, 'you are always with me, and everything I have is yours. [32] But we had to celebrate and rejoice, because this brother of yours was dead and is alive again; he was lost and is found.'"

Ephesians 1:7–8

[7] In him we have redemption through his blood,

the forgiveness of our trespasses, according to the riches of his grace [8] that he richly poured out on us with all wisdom and understanding.

RESPONSE

TIME   DATE

JESUS BRINGS JOY THROUGH REDEMPTION. WRITE A PRAYER OF GRATITUDE,
THANKING HIM FOR REDEEMING US FROM OUR WANDERING.

Joy

Joy

DAY
18

THROUGH

ABUNDANT

WEEK
03

Life

John 5:24–29

LIFE AND JUDGMENT

24 "Truly I tell you, anyone who hears my word and believes him who sent me has eternal life and will not come under judgment but has passed from death to life.

25 "Truly I tell you, an hour is coming, and is now here, when the dead will hear the voice of the Son of God, and those who hear will live. 26 For just as the Father has life in himself, so also he has granted to the Son to have life in himself. 27 And he has granted him the right to pass judgment, because he is the Son of Man. 28 Do not be amazed at this, because a time is coming when all who are in the graves will hear his voice 29 and come out—those who have done good things, to the resurrection of life, but those who have done wicked things, to the resurrection of condemnation."

John 10:7–18, 27–30

7 Jesus said again, "Truly I tell you, I am the gate for the sheep. 8 All who came before me are thieves and robbers, but the sheep didn't listen to them. 9 I am the gate. If anyone enters by me, he will be saved and will come in and go out and find pasture. 10 A thief comes only to steal and kill and destroy. I have come so that they may have life and have it in abundance.

11 "I am the good shepherd. The good shepherd lays down his life for the sheep. 12 The hired hand, since he is not the shepherd and doesn't own the sheep, leaves them and runs away when he sees a wolf coming. The wolf then snatches and scatters them. 13 This happens because he is a hired hand and doesn't care about the sheep.

14 "I am the good shepherd. I know my own, and my own know me, 15 just as the Father knows me, and I know the Father. I lay down my life for the sheep. 16 But I have other sheep that are not from this sheep pen; I must bring them also, and they will listen to my voice. Then there will be one flock, one shepherd. 17 This is why the Father loves me, because I lay down my life so that I may take it up again. 18 No one takes it from me, but I lay it down on my own. I have the right to lay it down, and I have the right to take it up again. I have received this command from my Father."

…

27 "My sheep hear my voice, I know them, and they follow me. 28 I give them eternal life, and they will never perish. No one will snatch them out of my hand. 29 My Father, who has given them to me, is greater than all. No one is able to snatch them out of the Father's hand. 30 I and the Father are one."

Notes

Psalm 16:5–11

⁵ LORD, you are my portion
and my cup of blessing;
you hold my future.

⁶ The boundary lines have fallen for me
in pleasant places;
indeed, I have a beautiful inheritance.

⁷ I will bless the Lord who counsels me—
even at night when my thoughts trouble me.
⁸ I always let the LORD guide me.
Because he is at my right hand,
I will not be shaken.

⁹ Therefore my heart is glad
and my whole being rejoices;
my body also rests securely.
¹⁰ For you will not abandon me to Sheol;
you will not allow your faithful one to see decay.
¹¹ You reveal the path of life to me;
in your presence is abundant joy;
at your right hand are eternal pleasures.

2 Peter 1:3–4

³ His divine power has given us everything required for life and godliness through the knowledge of him who called us by his own glory and goodness. ⁴ By these he has given us very great and precious promises, so that through them you may share in the divine nature, escaping the corruption that is in the world because of evil desire.

RESPONSE

TIME   DATE

JESUS BRINGS JOY THROUGH ABUNDANT LIFE. WRITE A PRAYER OF
GRATITUDE, THANKING HIM FOR PROVIDING ABUNDANT LIFE TO ALL
WHO FOLLOW HIM.

Joy

JOY THROUGH

"COME TO ME, ALL OF
YOU WHO ARE WEARY
AND BURDENED, AND I
WILL GIVE YOU REST."

MATTHEW 11:28

Rest

Isaiah 40:28–31

28 Do you not know?

Have you not heard?

The LORD is the everlasting God,

the Creator of the whole earth.

He never becomes faint or weary;

there is no limit to his understanding.

29 He gives strength to the faint

and strengthens the powerless.

30 Youths may become faint and weary,

and young men stumble and fall,

31 but those who trust in the LORD

will renew their strength;

they will soar on wings like eagles;

they will run and not become weary,

they will walk and not faint.

Psalm 23

THE GOOD SHEPHERD

A psalm of David.

1 The LORD is my shepherd;

I have what I need.

2 He lets me lie down in green pastures;

he leads me beside quiet waters.

3 He renews my life;

he leads me along the right paths

for his name's sake.

4 Even when I go through the darkest valley,

I fear no danger,

for you are with me;

your rod and your staff—they comfort me.

5 You prepare a table before me

in the presence of my enemies;

you anoint my head with oil;

my cup overflows.

6 Only goodness and faithful love will pursue me

all the days of my life,

and I will dwell in the house of the Lord

as long as I live.

Notes

Matthew 11:25–30

[25] At that time Jesus said, "I praise you, Father, Lord of heaven and earth, because you have hidden these things from the wise and intelligent and revealed them to infants. [26] Yes, Father, because this was your good pleasure. [27] All things have been entrusted to me by my Father. No one knows the Son except the Father, and no one knows the Father except the Son and anyone to whom the Son desires to reveal him.

[28] "Come to me, all of you who are weary and burdened, and I will give you rest. [29] Take my yoke upon you and learn from me, because I am lowly and humble in heart, and you will find rest for your souls. [30] For my yoke is easy and my burden is light."

Mark 6:30–31

[30] The apostles gathered around Jesus and reported to him all that they had done and taught. [31] He said to them, "Come away by yourselves to a remote place and rest for a while." For many people were coming and going, and they did not even have time to eat.

Revelation 14:13

Then I heard a voice from heaven saying, "Write: Blessed are the dead who die in the Lord from now on."

"Yes," says the Spirit, "so they will rest from their labors, since their works follow them."

DAY 19 — RESPONSE

TIME   DATE

JESUS BRINGS JOY THROUGH REST. WRITE A PRAYER OF GRATITUDE, THANKING
HIM FOR PROVIDING REST FOR OUR SOULS.

Joy

BREAKFAST
Casserole

INGREDIENTS

16 ounces breakfast sausage, ground

8 eggs

2 cups milk

3 cups cheddar cheese, shredded

1 teaspoon dry mustard

½ tablespoon onion powder

½ tablespoon garlic powder

1 teaspoon salt

1 teaspoon pepper

8 square hash browns

2 tablespoons parsley, chopped, for garnish

DIRECTIONS

Preheat oven to 350°F.

In a saute pan, cook sausage, breaking into crumbles with a spatula. Drain excess grease.

Whisk together eggs, milk, 2 cups of cheese, and seasonings. Mix until egg yolks and whites are fully incorporated.

Grease the sides and bottom of a 9 by 13-inch baking dish. Place one layer of hash browns on the bottom of baking dish. Distribute sausage evenly over hash browns. Pour egg mixture over hash browns and sausage. Can refrigerate overnight if desired.

Bake for 30 minutes, then spread remaining cup of cheese over top. Bake another 15 to 20 minutes, until cheese is golden and eggs are solid. Once cooled, sprinkle parsley over top, and cut into squares.

PREP TIME	COOK TIME	YIELD
10 minutes	45–50 minutes	12 servings

Joy THROUGH Humility

Luke 1:26–56

GABRIEL PREDICTS JESUS'S BIRTH

[26] In the sixth month, the angel Gabriel was sent by God to a town in Galilee called Nazareth, [27] to a virgin engaged to a man named Joseph, of the house of David. The virgin's name was Mary. [28] And the angel came to her and said, "Greetings, favored woman! The Lord is with you." [29] But she was deeply troubled by this statement, wondering what kind of greeting this could be. [30] Then the angel told her, "Do not be afraid, Mary, for you have found favor with God. [31] Now listen: You will conceive and give birth to a son, and you will name him Jesus. [32] He will be great and will be called the Son of the Most High, and the Lord God will give him the throne of his father David. [33] He will reign over the house of Jacob forever, and his kingdom will have no end."

[34] Mary asked the angel, "How can this be, since I have not had sexual relations with a man?"

[35] The angel replied to her, "The Holy Spirit will come upon you, and the power of the Most High will overshadow you. Therefore, the holy one to be born will be called the Son of God. [36] And consider your relative Elizabeth—even she has conceived a son in her old age, and this is the sixth month for her who was called childless. [37] For nothing will be impossible with God."

[38] "See, I am the Lord's servant," said Mary. "May it happen to me as you have said." Then the angel left her.

MARY'S VISIT TO ELIZABETH

[39] In those days Mary set out and hurried to a town in the hill country of Judah [40] where she entered Zechariah's house and greeted Elizabeth. [41] When Elizabeth heard Mary's greeting, the baby leaped inside her, and Elizabeth was filled with the Holy Spirit. [42] Then she exclaimed with a loud cry, "Blessed are you among women, and your child will be

blessed! [43] How could this happen to me, that the mother of my Lord should come to me? [44] For you see, when the sound of your greeting reached my ears, the baby leaped for joy inside me. [45] Blessed is she who has believed that the Lord would fulfill what he has spoken to her!"

MARY'S PRAISE

[46] And Mary said:

> My soul magnifies the Lord,
> [47] and my spirit rejoices in God my Savior,
> [48] because he has looked with favor
> on the humble condition of his servant.
> Surely, from now on all generations
> will call me blessed,
> [49] because the Mighty One
> has done great things for me,
> and his name is holy.
> [50] His mercy is from generation to generation
> on those who fear him.
> [51] He has done a mighty deed with his arm;
> he has scattered the proud
> because of the thoughts of their hearts;
> [52] he has toppled the mighty from their thrones
> and exalted the lowly.
> [53] He has satisfied the hungry with good things
> and sent the rich away empty.
> [54] He has helped his servant Israel,
> remembering his mercy
> [55] to Abraham and his descendants forever,
> just as he spoke to our ancestors.

[56] And Mary stayed with her about three months; then she returned to her home.

Psalm 131

A CHILDLIKE SPIRIT

A song of ascents. Of David.

[1] Lord, my heart is not proud;
my eyes are not haughty.
I do not get involved with things
too great or too wondrous for me.
[2] Instead, I have calmed and quieted my soul
like a weaned child with its mother;
my soul is like a weaned child.

[3] Israel, put your hope in the LORD,
both now and forever.

Philippians 2:5–11

CHRIST'S HUMILITY AND EXALTATION

[5] Adopt the same attitude as that of Christ Jesus,

[6] who, existing in the form of God,
did not consider equality with God
as something to be exploited.
[7] Instead he emptied himself
by assuming the form of a servant,
taking on the likeness of humanity.
And when he had come as a man,
[8] he humbled himself by becoming obedient
to the point of death—
even to death on a cross.
[9] For this reason God highly exalted him
and gave him the name
that is above every name,
[10] so that at the name of Jesus
every knee will bow—
in heaven and on earth
and under the earth—
[11] and every tongue will confess
that Jesus Christ is Lord,
to the glory of God the Father.

James 4:6–10

[6] But he gives greater grace. Therefore he says:

God resists the proud
but gives grace to the humble.

[7] Therefore, submit to God. Resist the devil, and he will flee from you. [8] Draw near to God, and he will draw near to you. Cleanse your hands, sinners, and purify your hearts, you double-minded. [9] Be miserable and mourn and weep. Let your laughter be turned to mourning and your joy to gloom. [10] Humble yourselves before the Lord, and he will exalt you.

RESPONSE

TIME   DATE

JESUS BRINGS JOY THROUGH HUMILITY. WRITE A PRAYER
OF GRATITUDE, THANKING HIM FOR EXALTING THE HUMBLE.

Joy

DAY 21

GRACE *Day*

TAKE THIS DAY TO CATCH UP ON
YOUR READING, PRAY, AND REST
IN THE PRESENCE OF THE LORD.

*A*ND WE HAVE SEEN AND
WE TESTIFY THAT THE
FATHER HAS SENT HIS SON
AS THE WORLD'S SAVIOR.

1 JOHN 4:14

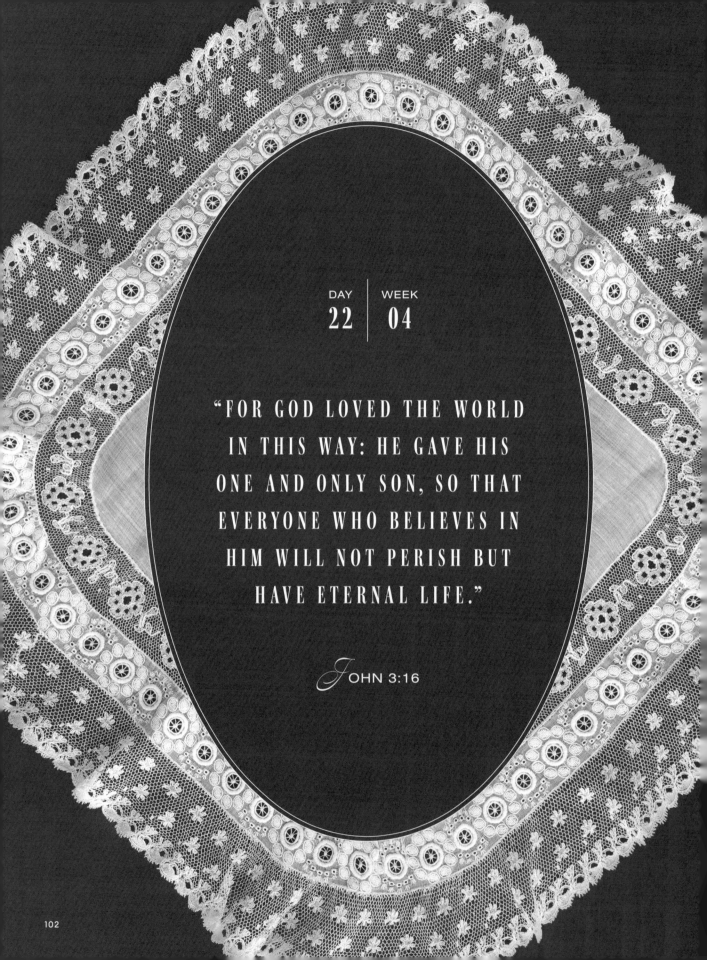

DAY | WEEK
22 | **04**

"FOR GOD LOVED THE WORLD
IN THIS WAY: HE GAVE HIS
ONE AND ONLY SON, SO THAT
EVERYONE WHO BELIEVES IN
HIM WILL NOT PERISH BUT
HAVE ETERNAL LIFE."

*J*OHN 3:16

THE
FOURTH SUNDAY
OF
ADVENT:

As Christmas Day approaches, we turn our attention to the great love that prompted God to send His one and only Son to earth. We see the love of God—His affection, care, and kindness to His children—on display through each part of His Son's arrival. In this week's readings, we will look at some of the specific ways that God showed His people the kind of love that prompted Simeon's praise: "My eyes have seen your salvation. You have prepared it in the presence of all peoples" (Lk 2:30–31).

The title of each day of reading this week completes the statement "Jesus is…"

CHRISTMAS MORNING *Waffles*

INGREDIENTS

2 cups flour

2 teaspoons sugar

½ teaspoon salt

4 teaspoons baking powder

1¾ cups milk

2 eggs, separated

½ cup butter, melted

DIRECTIONS

Sift dry ingredients together.

Whisk milk and egg yolks, then add to dry ingredients. Stir in melted butter until all lumps have disappeared and the texture is smooth and creamy. Using an electric mixer, beat egg whites until soft peaks form, then fold into batter.

Brush waffle iron with additional melted butter and preheat. Pour in batter and let cook about 3 minutes, or until steam has stopped coming out of the iron. Repeat with remaining batter, brushing waffle iron with butter each time. Serve piping hot with your favorite toppings.

PREP TIME	COOK TIME	YIELD
15 minutes	35–40 minutes	12 servings

LOVE
Foretold

Luke 1:5–25, 57–80

GABRIEL PREDICTS JOHN'S BIRTH

[5] In the days of King Herod of Judea, there was a priest of Abijah's division named Zechariah. His wife was from the daughters of Aaron, and her name was Elizabeth. [6] Both were righteous in God's sight, living without blame according to all the commands and requirements of the Lord. [7] But they had no children because Elizabeth could not conceive, and both of them were well along in years.

[8] When his division was on duty and he was serving as priest before God, [9] it happened that he was chosen by lot, according to the custom of the priesthood, to enter the sanctuary of the Lord and burn incense. [10] At the hour of incense the whole assembly of the people was praying outside. [11] An angel of the Lord appeared to him, standing to the right of the altar of incense. [12] When Zechariah saw him, he was terrified and overcome with fear. [13] But the angel said to him, "Do not be afraid, Zechariah, because your prayer has been heard. Your wife Elizabeth will bear you a son, and you will name him John. [14] There will be joy and delight for you, and many will rejoice at his birth. [15] For he will be great in the sight of the Lord and will never drink wine or beer. He will be filled

with the Holy Spirit while still in his mother's womb. [16] He will turn many of the children of Israel to the Lord their God. [17] And he will go before him in the spirit and power of Elijah, to turn the hearts of fathers to their children, and the disobedient to the understanding of the righteous, to make ready for the Lord a prepared people."

[18] "How can I know this?" Zechariah asked the angel. "For I am an old man, and my wife is well along in years."

[19] The angel answered him, "I am Gabriel, who stands in the presence of God, and I was sent to speak to you and tell you this good news. [20] Now listen. You will become silent and unable to speak until the day these things take place, because you did not believe my words, which will be fulfilled in their proper time."

[21] Meanwhile, the people were waiting for Zechariah, amazed that he stayed so long in the sanctuary. [22] When he did come out, he could not speak to them. Then they realized that he had seen a vision in the sanctuary. He was making signs

to them and remained speechless. ²³ When the days of his ministry were completed, he went back home.

²⁴ After these days his wife Elizabeth conceived and kept herself in seclusion for five months. She said, ²⁵ "The Lord has done this for me. He has looked with favor in these days to take away my disgrace among the people."

…

THE BIRTH AND NAMING OF JOHN
⁵⁷ Now the time had come for Elizabeth to give birth, and she had a son. ⁵⁸ Then her neighbors and relatives heard that the Lord had shown her his great mercy, and they rejoiced with her.

⁵⁹ When they came to circumcise the child on the eighth day, they were going to name him Zechariah, after his father. ⁶⁰ But his mother responded, "No. He will be called John."

⁶¹ Then they said to her, "None of your relatives has that name." ⁶² So they motioned to his father to find out what he wanted him to be called. ⁶³ He asked for a writing tablet and wrote, "His name is John." And they were all amazed. ⁶⁴ Immediately his mouth was opened and his tongue set free, and he began to speak, praising God. ⁶⁵ Fear came on all those who lived around them, and all these things were being talked about throughout the hill country of Judea. ⁶⁶ All who heard about him took it to heart, saying, "What then will this child become?" For, indeed, the Lord's hand was with him.

ZECHARIAH'S PROPHECY
⁶⁷ Then his father Zechariah was filled with the Holy Spirit and prophesied:

⁶⁸ Blessed is the Lord, the God of Israel,
because he has visited
and provided redemption for his people.
⁶⁹ He has raised up a horn of salvation for us
in the house of his servant David,
⁷⁰ just as he spoke by the mouth
of his holy prophets in ancient times;
⁷¹ salvation from our enemies
and from the hand of those who hate us.

⁷² He has dealt mercifully with our ancestors
and remembered his holy covenant—
⁷³ the oath that he swore to our father Abraham,
to grant that we,
⁷⁴ having been rescued
from the hand of our enemies,
would serve him without fear
⁷⁵ in holiness and righteousness
in his presence all our days.
⁷⁶ And you, child, will be called
a prophet of the Most High,
for you will go before the Lord
to prepare his ways,
⁷⁷ to give his people knowledge of salvation
through the forgiveness of their sins.
⁷⁸ Because of our God's merciful compassion,
the dawn from on high will visit us
⁷⁹ to shine on those who live in darkness
and the shadow of death,
to guide our feet into the way of peace.

⁸⁰ The child grew up and became strong in spirit, and he was in the wilderness until the day of his public appearance to Israel.

Matthew 11:1–15
JOHN THE BAPTIST DOUBTS
¹ When Jesus had finished giving instructions to his twelve disciples, he moved on from there to teach and preach in their towns. ² Now when John heard in prison what the Christ was doing, he sent a message through his disciples ³ and asked him, "Are you the one who is to come, or should we expect someone else?"

⁴ Jesus replied to them, "Go and report to John what you hear and see: ⁵ The blind receive their sight, the lame walk, those with leprosy are cleansed, the deaf hear, the dead are raised, and the poor are told the good news, ⁶ and blessed is the one who isn't offended by me."

⁷ As these men were leaving, Jesus began to speak to the crowds about John: "What did you go out into the wilderness to see? A reed swaying in the wind? ⁸ What then did you go

out to see? A man dressed in soft clothes? See, those who wear soft clothes are in royal palaces. ⁹ What then did you go out to see? A prophet? Yes, I tell you, and more than a prophet. ¹⁰ This is the one about whom it is written:

> See, I am sending my messenger ahead of you;
> he will prepare your way before you.

¹¹ "Truly I tell you, among those born of women no one greater than John the Baptist has appeared, but the least in the kingdom of heaven is greater than he. ¹² From the days of John the Baptist until now, the kingdom of heaven has been suffering violence, and the violent have been seizing it by force. ¹³ For all the prophets and the law prophesied until John. ¹⁴ And if you're willing to accept it, he is the Elijah who is to come. ¹⁵ Let anyone who has ears listen."

Hebrews 1:1–2

¹ Long ago God spoke to our ancestors by the prophets at different times and in different ways. ² In these last days, he has spoken to us by his Son. God has appointed him heir of all things and made the universe through him.

1 Peter 2:9–10

⁹ But you are a chosen race, a royal priesthood, a holy nation, a people for his possession, so that you may proclaim the praises of the one who called you out of darkness into his marvelous light. ¹⁰ Once you were not a people, but now you are God's people;

you had not received mercy, but now you have received mercy.

RESPONSE

TIME

DATE

As you respond this week, consider praying about how each day's reading leads you to praise, shapes your perspective on what it means to love and be loved, and equips you to encourage those in your community.

JESUS IS LOVE FORETOLD. WRITE A PRAYER OF GRATITUDE, THANKING HIM FOR BEING THE EMBODIMENT OF GOD'S COMPASSION TOWARD US.

Love

THE
Incarnation

The Advent season is a reflection on the wonderful reality of the incarnation, when God took on human nature and flesh. In Jesus, we find the embodiment of God, the Son who is both fully God and fully human and came to dwell with us. In this extra you will find helpful biblical and historical context surrounding the incarnation.

THE INCARNATION IN SCRIPTURE

KEY PASSAGES

…See, the virgin will conceive, have a son, and name him Immanuel.
Is 7:14

…Jesus also was baptized. As he was praying, heaven opened….And a voice came from heaven: "You are my beloved Son; with you I am well-pleased."
Lk 3:21–22

"I and the Father are one."
Jn 10:30

When the time came to completion, God sent his Son, born of a woman, born under the law, to redeem those under the law, so that we might receive adoption as sons.
Gl 4:4–5

Instead he emptied himself by assuming the form of a servant, taking on the likeness of humanity. And when he had come as a man, he humbled himself…
Php 2:7–8

He is the image of the invisible God, the firstborn over all creation…. For God was pleased to have all his fullness dwell in him…
Col 1:15, 19

The Son is the radiance of God's glory and the exact expression of his nature, sustaining all things by his powerful word.
Heb 1:3

JESUS AS SON

Throughout the New Testament, Jesus is referred to as "the son of" several different entities. The titles listed here are a few that are particularly helpful for understanding the incarnation.

THE SON OF GOD
──────────────────

Mt 16:15–16; Mk 1:1; 3:11; Jn 5:17–23

This title was used by New Testament authors, believers, unclean spirits, God the Father, and Jesus Himself. It explains the relationship between the first two persons of the Trinity—God the Father and God the Son. The title is a reminder that Jesus has the right and authority to carry out God's purposes, since the fullness of God dwells in Him.

THE SON OF MARY
──────────────────

Gn 3:15; Mt 1:16; Mk 6:3; Lk 1:26–38

In the garden of Eden, after Adam and Eve sinned, God declared that there would be hostility between the offspring of the serpent and the woman. Jesus is the foretold descendant of Eve, born of another woman, Mary. He ultimately struck the enemy down once and for all through His death, resurrection, ascension.

THE SON OF JOSEPH
──────────────────

Mt 1:18–25; Lk 4:22; Jn 1:45

Jesus was raised by His earthly father, Joseph. It is through Joseph's family line that we trace Jesus's ancestry, situating Him in the human lineage of both Adam and Abraham.

THE INCARNATION IN CHURCH HISTORY

HERESIES ABOUT THE INCARNATION

A heresy is a conscious deviation from the traditionally held, widely-accepted teaching. As the early Church grew and spread, heresies arose that contradicted the teachings of the apostles. Here is a summary of some of the most influential heresies that strayed from the truth of Jesus's incarnation.

MARCIONISM

Seeing God in the Old Testament as full of wrath and vengeance, Marcion (a bishop born around AD 85 who was excommunicated from the Church for his views) concluded that the God of the New Testament, revealed by His Son, Jesus, must be a superior and altogether separate deity. In Marcion thought, Jesus was not actually human, but only appeared in human form.

DOCETISM

Docetism is the belief that Christ only seemed to have a physical body. (Docetism comes from the Greek word *dokein*, "to seem.") As in Marcionism, the idea is that since Christ is God, He could not possibly be contained in a physical body. What was seen as Jesus's body was actually only an illusion or phantom.

MODALISM

Modalism presumes that since there is one God, He cannot exist in three persons. Instead, the Father, Son, and the Holy Spirit are three manifestations, or modes, of God. To put it another way, Yahweh of the Old Testament became Jesus in the Gospels and later the Holy Spirit who indwells believers.

ARIANISM

Arius, a minister born around AD 250, taught that Jesus was a created being and therefore inferior to God the Father—meaning that there was a time before the Son came into being when the Father existed on His own. According to Arius, God the Father alone is infinite and Jesus was made God by the will and permission of the Father. In addition, the Holy Spirit was created by the Father with the help of the Son and is inferior to both.

THE NICENE CREED

In response to these heresies, councils formed to create unity and define what the church believed about key doctrines. These councils formed creeds that served as a rule of faith, one of which was the Nicene Creed that was written at the First Council of Nicea in AD 325 in response to Arianism. Here is an excerpt from this creed which stands today as one of the most widely-accepted statements of belief about the incarnation.

We believe....in one Lord Jesus Christ,
   the only Son of God,
   begotten from the Father before all ages,
     God from God,
     Light from Light,
     true God from true God,
   begotten, not made;
   of the same essence as the Father.
   Through him all things were made.
   For us and for our salvation
     he came down from heaven;
     he became incarnate by the Holy Spirit
      and the virgin Mary,
   and was made human.
   He was crucified for us under Pontius Pilate;
   he suffered and was buried.
   The third day he rose again, according to
     the Scriptures.
   He ascended to heaven
   and is seated at the right hand of the Father.
   He will come again with glory
   to judge the living and the dead.
   His kingdom will never end.

Love COME **NEAR**

DAY
24

WEEK
04

Christmas Eve

Matthew 1:1–25

THE GENEALOGY OF JESUS CHRIST

¹ An account of the genealogy of Jesus Christ, the Son of David, the Son of Abraham:

FROM ABRAHAM TO DAVID

² Abraham fathered Isaac,
Isaac fathered Jacob,
Jacob fathered Judah and his brothers,
³ Judah fathered Perez and Zerah by Tamar,
Perez fathered Hezron,
Hezron fathered Aram,
⁴ Aram fathered Amminadab,
Amminadab fathered Nahshon,
Nahshon fathered Salmon,
⁵ Salmon fathered Boaz by Rahab,
Boaz fathered Obed by Ruth,
Obed fathered Jesse,
⁶ and Jesse fathered King David.

FROM DAVID TO THE BABYLONIAN EXILE

David fathered Solomon by Uriah's wife,
⁷ Solomon fathered Rehoboam,
Rehoboam fathered Abijah,
Abijah fathered Asa,
⁸ Asa fathered Jehoshaphat,
Jehoshaphat fathered Joram,
Joram fathered Uzziah,
⁹ Uzziah fathered Jotham,
Jotham fathered Ahaz,
Ahaz fathered Hezekiah,
¹⁰ Hezekiah fathered Manasseh,
Manasseh fathered Amon,
Amon fathered Josiah,
¹¹ and Josiah fathered Jeconiah and his brothers at the time of the exile to Babylon.

FROM THE EXILE TO THE MESSIAH

¹² After the exile to Babylon
Jeconiah fathered Shealtiel,
Shealtiel fathered Zerubbabel,
¹³ Zerubbabel fathered Abiud,
Abiud fathered Eliakim,
Eliakim fathered Azor,
¹⁴ Azor fathered Zadok,
Zadok fathered Achim,
Achim fathered Eliud,
¹⁵ Eliud fathered Eleazar,
Eleazar fathered Matthan,
Matthan fathered Jacob,
¹⁶ and Jacob fathered Joseph the husband of Mary, who gave birth to Jesus who is called the Messiah.

¹⁷ So all the generations from Abraham to David were fourteen generations; and from David until the exile to Babylon, fourteen generations; and from the exile to Babylon until the Messiah, fourteen generations.

THE NATIVITY OF THE MESSIAH

¹⁸ The birth of Jesus Christ came about this way: After his mother Mary had been engaged to Joseph, it was discovered before they came together that she was pregnant from the Holy Spirit. ¹⁹ So her husband, Joseph, being a righteous man, and not wanting to disgrace her publicly, decided to divorce her secretly.

²⁰ But after he had considered these things, an angel of the Lord appeared to him in a dream, saying, "Joseph, son of David, don't be afraid to take Mary as your wife, because what has been conceived in her is from the Holy Spirit. ²¹ She will give birth to a son, and you are to name him Jesus, because he will save his people from their sins."

²² Now all this took place to fulfill what was spoken by the Lord through the prophet:

²³ See, the virgin will become pregnant
and give birth to a son,
and they will name him Immanuel,

which is translated "God is with us."

²⁴ When Joseph woke up, he did as the Lord's angel had commanded him. He married her ²⁵ but did not have sexual relations with her until she gave birth to a son. And he named him Jesus.

John 1:14–18

[14] The Word became flesh and dwelt among us. We observed his glory, the glory as the one and only Son from the Father, full of grace and truth. [15] (John testified concerning him and exclaimed, "This was the one of whom I said, 'The one coming after me ranks ahead of me, because he existed before me.'") [16] Indeed, we have all received grace upon grace from his fullness, [17] for the law was given through Moses; grace and truth came through Jesus Christ.

[18] No one has ever seen God. The one and only Son, who is himself God and is at the Father's side—he has revealed him.

Galatians 4:4–5

[4] When the time came to completion, God sent his Son, born of a woman, born under the law, [5] to redeem those under the law, so that we might receive adoption as sons.

RESPONSE

JESUS IS LOVE COME NEAR. WRITE A PRAYER OF GRATITUDE,
THANKING HIM FOR COMING TO BE GOD WITH US.

Love

Silent NIGHT, HOLY Night

WORDS

Joseph Mohr; stanzas 1 and 3 translated by John Freeman
Young; stanzas 2 and 4 translated by anonymous

MUSIC

Franz Grüber

1. Si - lent night, ho - ly night, All is calm, all is bright
2. Si - lent night, ho - ly night, Dark - ness flies, all is light;
3. Si - lent night, ho - ly night, Son of God, love's pure light
4. Si - lent night, ho - ly night, Won - drous star, lend thy light;

Round yon vir - gin moth - er and child! Ho - ly In - fant so ten - der and
Shep - herds hear the an - gels sing, "Al - le - lu - ia! hail the
Ra - diant beams from Thy ho - ly face, With the dawn of re - deem - ing
With the an - gels let us sing al - le - lu - ia to our

mild, Sleep in heav - en - ly peace, Sleep in heav - en - ly peace.
King! Christ the Sav - ior is born, Christ the Sav - ior is born."
grace, Je - sus, Lord, at Thy birth, Je - sus, Lord, at Thy birth.
King; Christ the Sav - ior is born, Christ the Sav - ior is born.

CHRISTMAS
Day

TODAY IN THE CITY OF
DAVID A SAVIOR WAS BORN
FOR YOU, WHO IS THE
MESSIAH, THE LORD.

*L*UKE 2:11

Love

DAY
25

IN A

WEEK
04

Manger

NOTES

Micah 5:2

Bethlehem Ephrathah,
you are small among the clans of Judah;
one will come from you
to be ruler over Israel for me.
His origin is from antiquity,
from ancient times.

Luke 2:1–20

THE BIRTH OF JESUS

[1] In those days a decree went out from Caesar Augustus that the whole empire should be registered. [2] This first registration took place while Quirinius was governing Syria. [3] So everyone went to be registered, each to his own town.

[4] Joseph also went up from the town of Nazareth in Galilee, to Judea, to the city of David, which is called Bethlehem, because he was of the house and family line of David, [5] to be registered along with Mary, who was engaged to him and was pregnant. [6] While they were there, the time came for her to give birth. [7] Then she gave birth to her firstborn son, and she wrapped him tightly in cloth and laid him in a manger, because there was no guest room available for them.

THE SHEPHERDS AND THE ANGELS

[8] In the same region, shepherds were staying out in the fields and keeping watch at night over their flock. [9] Then an angel of the Lord stood before them, and the glory of the Lord shone around them, and they were terrified. [10] But the angel said to them, "Don't be afraid, for look, I proclaim to you good news of great joy that will be for all the people: [11] Today in the city of David a Savior was born for you, who is the Messiah, the Lord. [12] This will be the sign for you: You will find a baby wrapped tightly in cloth and lying in a manger."

[13] Suddenly there was a multitude of the heavenly host with the angel, praising God and saying:

[14] Glory to God in the highest heaven,
and peace on earth to people he favors!

[15] When the angels had left them and returned to heaven, the shepherds said to one another, "Let's go straight to Bethlehem and see what has happened, which the Lord has made known to us."

[16] They hurried off and found both Mary and Joseph, and the baby who was lying in the manger. [17] After seeing them, they reported the message they were told about this child, [18] and all who heard it were amazed at what the shepherds said to them. [19] But Mary was treasuring up all these things in her heart and meditating on them. [20] The shepherds returned, glorifying and praising God for all the things they had seen and heard, which were just as they had been told.

CHRISTMAS *Day* REFLECTION

WHERE DID I SPEND CHRISTMAS DAY?

WHAT TIME DID I WAKE UP?

AM / PM

WHAT WAS THE WEATHER LIKE?

WHO DID I CELEBRATE WITH?

WHAT MADE ME LAUGH?

WHAT SENSE OF LOSS, GRIEF, OR UNMET EXPECTATIONS DID I
EXPERIENCE TODAY?

HOW DID I EXPERIENCE THE NEARNESS OF GOD TODAY?

WHAT'S ONE MEMORY FROM TODAY THAT I WILL CARRY WITH ME?

HOW WAS CHRISTMAS DAY DIFFERENT THIS YEAR BECAUSE OF
THE TIME I SPENT READING GOD'S WORD DURING ADVENT?

LOVE

FOR MY
EYES HAVE
SEEN YOUR
SALVATION.

LUKE 2:30

Proclaimed

Isaiah 49:5–6

5 And now, says the LORD,

who formed me from the womb to be his servant,

to bring Jacob back to him

so that Israel might be gathered to him;

for I am honored in the sight of the LORD,

and my God is my strength—

6 he says,

"It is not enough for you to be my servant

raising up the tribes of Jacob

and restoring the protected ones of Israel.

I will also make you a light for the nations, to be my salvation to the ends of the earth."

Luke 2:21–40

THE CIRCUMCISION AND PRESENTATION OF JESUS

21 When the eight days were completed for his circumcision, he was named Jesus—the name given by the angel before he was conceived. 22 And when the days of their purification according to the law of Moses were finished, they brought him up to Jerusalem to present him to the Lord 23 (just as it is written in the law of the Lord, Every firstborn male will be dedicated to the Lord) 24 and to offer a sacrifice (according to what is stated in the law of the Lord, a pair of turtledoves or two young pigeons).

SIMEON'S PROPHETIC PRAISE

25 There was a man in Jerusalem whose name was Simeon. This man was righteous and devout, looking forward to Israel's consolation, and the Holy Spirit was on him. 26 It had been revealed to him by the Holy Spirit that he would not see death before he saw the Lord's Messiah. 27 Guided by the Spirit, he entered the temple. When the parents brought in the child Jesus to perform for him what was customary under the law, 28 Simeon took him up in his arms, praised God, and said,

29 Now, Master,

you can dismiss your servant in peace,

as you promised.

30 For my eyes have seen your salvation.

31 You have prepared it

in the presence of all peoples—

32 a light for revelation to the Gentiles

and glory to your people Israel.

[33] His father and mother were amazed at what was being said about him. [34] Then Simeon blessed them and told his mother Mary, "Indeed, this child is destined to cause the fall and rise of many in Israel and to be a sign that will be opposed— [35] and a sword will pierce your own soul—that the thoughts of many hearts may be revealed."

ANNA'S TESTIMONY
[36] There was also a prophetess, Anna, a daughter of Phanuel, of the tribe of Asher. She was well along in years, having lived with her husband seven years after her marriage, [37] and was a widow for eighty-four years. She did not leave the temple, serving God night and day with fasting and prayers. [38] At that very moment, she came up and began to thank God and to speak about him to all who were looking forward to the redemption of Jerusalem.

THE FAMILY'S RETURN TO NAZARETH
[39] When they had completed everything according to the law of the Lord, they returned to Galilee, to their own town of Nazareth. [40] The boy grew up and became strong, filled with wisdom, and God's grace was on him.

RESPONSE

TIME   DATE

JESUS IS LOVE PROCLAIMED. WRITE A PRAYER OF GRATITUDE,
THANKING HIM FOR EXTENDING HIS LOVE TO ALL PEOPLE.

Love

DAY 27 ═══   ═══ WEEK 04

Love DISPLAYED

John 3:16

"For God loved the world in this way: He gave his one and only Son, so that everyone who believes in him will not perish but have eternal life."

1 Corinthians 13

LOVE: THE SUPERIOR WAY

[1] If I speak human or angelic tongues but do not have love, I am a noisy gong or a clanging cymbal. [2] If I have the gift of prophecy and understand all mysteries and all knowledge, and if I have all faith so that I can move mountains but do not have love, I am nothing. [3] And if I give away all my possessions, and if I give over my body in order to boast but do not have love, I gain nothing.

[4] Love is patient, love is kind. Love does not envy, is not boastful, is not arrogant, [5] is not rude, is not self-seeking, is not irritable, and does not keep a record of wrongs. [6] Love finds no joy in unrighteousness but rejoices in the truth. [7] It bears all things, believes all things, hopes all things, endures all things.

[8] Love never ends. But as for prophecies, they will come to an end; as for tongues, they will cease; as for knowledge, it will come to an end. [9] For we know in part, and we prophesy in part, [10] but when the perfect comes, the partial will come to an end. [11] When I was a child, I spoke like a child, I thought like a child, I reasoned like a child. When I became a man, I put aside childish things. [12] For now we see only a reflection as in a mirror, but then face to face. Now I know in part, but then I will know fully, as I am fully known. [13] Now these three remain: faith, hope, and love—but the greatest of these is love.

1 John 4:9–10

[9] God's love was revealed among us in this way: God sent his one and only Son into the world so that we might live through him. [10] Love consists in this: not that we loved God, but that he loved us and sent his Son to be the atoning sacrifice for our sins.

John 13:1–17

JESUS WASHES HIS DISCIPLES' FEET

[1] Before the Passover Festival, Jesus knew that his hour had come to depart from this world to the Father. Having loved his own who were in the world, he loved them to the end.

[2] Now when it was time for supper, the devil had already put it into the heart of Judas, Simon Iscariot's son, to betray him. [3] Jesus knew that the Father had given everything into his hands, that he had come from God, and that he was going back to God. [4] So he got up from supper, laid aside his outer clothing, took a towel, and tied it around himself. [5] Next, he poured water into a basin and began to wash his disciples' feet and to dry them with the towel tied around him.

[6] He came to Simon Peter, who asked him, "Lord, are you going to wash my feet?"

[7] Jesus answered him, "What I'm doing you don't realize now, but afterward you will understand."

[8] "You will never wash my feet," Peter said.

Jesus replied, "If I don't wash you, you have no part with me."

[9] Simon Peter said to him, "Lord, not only my feet, but also my hands and my head."

[10] "One who has bathed," Jesus told him, "doesn't need to wash anything except his feet, but he is completely clean. You are clean, but not all of you." [11] For he knew who would betray him. This is why he said, "Not all of you are clean."

THE MEANING OF FOOT WASHING

[12] When Jesus had washed their feet and put on his outer clothing, he reclined again and said to them, "Do you know what I have done for you? [13] You call me Teacher and Lord—and you are speaking rightly, since that is what I am. [14] So

if I, your Lord and Teacher, have washed your feet, you also ought to wash one another's feet. [15] For I have given you an example, that you also should do just as I have done for you.

[16] "Truly I tell you, a servant is not greater than his master, and a messenger is not greater than the one who sent him. [17] If you know these things, you are blessed if you do them."

John 15:9-17
CHRISTLIKE LOVE

[9] "As the Father has loved me, I have also loved you.

Remain in my love. [10] If you keep my commands you will remain in my love, just as I have kept my Father's commands and remain in his love.

[11] "I have told you these things so that my joy may be in you and your joy may be complete.

[12] "This is my command: Love one another as I have loved you. [13] No one has greater love than this: to lay down his life for his friends. [14] You are my friends if you do what I command you. [15] I do not call you servants anymore, because a servant doesn't know what his master is doing. I have called you friends, because I have made known to you everything I have heard from my Father. [16] You did not choose me, but I chose you. I appointed you to go and produce fruit and that your fruit should remain, so that whatever you ask the Father in my name, he will give you.

[17] "This is what I command you: Love one another."

1 John 3:1
See what great love the Father has given us that we should be called God's children—and we are! The reason the world does not know us is that it didn't know him.

DAY 27 · **RESPONSE**

TIME   DATE

JESUS IS LOVE DISPLAYED. WRITE A PRAYER
OF GRATITUDE, THANKING HIM FOR SHOWING US TRUE LOVE.

Love

GRACE *Day*

TAKE THIS DAY TO CATCH UP ON
YOUR READING, PRAY, AND REST
IN THE PRESENCE OF THE LORD.

*W*HEN THE TIME CAME TO COMPLETION, GOD SENT HIS SON, BORN OF A WOMAN, BORN UNDER THE LAW, TO REDEEM THOSE UNDER THE LAW, SO THAT WE MIGHT RECEIVE ADOPTION AS SONS.

GALATIANS 4:4–5

DAY | WEEK
29 | **05**

BUT THANKS BE TO
GOD, WHO GIVES US THE
VICTORY THROUGH OUR
LORD JESUS CHRIST!

1 CORINTHIANS 15:57

THE
FIRST SUNDAY
OF
CHRISTMASTIDE:

Rejoice

Each week we have looked at how Jesus came to be and bring the hope, peace, joy, and love of His kingdom to earth. In response, we rejoice in all Jesus has already accomplished, proclaiming His good news to the world. In this week's readings, we will look at some of the specific ways we can rejoice by modeling Jesus's example in how we live according to the hope, peace, joy, and love that He brought.

WE *Rejoice* IN GOD'S *Kingdom*

Daniel 2:27–45

[27] Daniel answered the king, "No wise man, medium, magician, or diviner is able to make known to the king the mystery he asked about. [28] But there is a God in heaven who reveals mysteries, and he has let King Nebuchadnezzar know what will happen in the last days. Your dream and the visions that came into your mind as you lay in bed were these: [29] Your Majesty, while you were in your bed, thoughts came to your mind about what will happen in the future. The revealer of mysteries has let you know what will happen. [30] As for me, this mystery has been revealed to me, not because I have more wisdom than anyone living, but in order that the interpretation might be made known to the king, and that you may understand the thoughts of your mind.

THE DREAM'S INTERPRETATION

[31] "Your Majesty, as you were watching, suddenly a colossal statue appeared. That statue, tall and dazzling, was standing in front of you, and its appearance was terrifying. [32] The head of the statue was pure gold, its chest and arms were silver, its stomach and thighs were bronze, [33] its legs were iron, and its feet were partly iron and partly fired clay. [34] As you were watching, a stone broke off without a hand touching it, struck the statue on its feet of iron and fired clay, and crushed them. [35] Then the iron, the fired clay, the bronze, the silver, and the gold were shattered and became like chaff from the summer threshing floors. The wind carried them away, and not a trace of them could be found. But the stone that struck the statue became a great mountain and filled the whole earth.

[36] "This was the dream; now we will tell the king its interpretation. [37] Your Majesty, you are king of kings. The God of the heavens has given you sovereignty, power, strength, and glory. [38] Wherever people live—or wild animals, or birds of the sky—he has handed them over to you and made you ruler over them all. You are the head of gold.

[39] "After you, there will arise another kingdom, inferior to yours, and then another, a third kingdom, of bronze, which will rule the whole earth. [40] A fourth kingdom will be as strong as iron; for iron crushes and shatters everything, and like iron that smashes, it will crush and smash all the others. [41] You saw the feet and toes, partly of a potter's fired clay and partly of iron—it will be a divided kingdom, though some of the strength of iron will be in it. You saw the iron mixed with clay, [42] and that the toes of the feet were partly iron and partly fired clay—part of the kingdom will be strong, and part will be brittle. [43] You saw the iron mixed with clay—the peoples will mix with one another but will not hold together, just as iron does not mix with fired clay.

⁴⁴ "In the days of those kings, the God of the heavens will set up a kingdom that will never be destroyed, and this kingdom will not be left to another people. It will crush all these kingdoms and bring them to an end, but will itself endure forever. ⁴⁵ You saw a stone break off from the mountain without a hand touching it, and it crushed the iron, bronze, fired clay, silver, and gold. The great God has told the king what will happen in the future. The dream is certain, and its interpretation reliable."

Daniel 7.13–14

¹³ I continued watching in the night visions,

and suddenly one like a son of man
was coming with the clouds of heaven.
He approached the Ancient of Days
and was escorted before him.
¹⁴ He was given dominion
and glory and a kingdom,
so that those of every people,
nation, and language
should serve him.
His dominion is an everlasting dominion
that will not pass away,
and his kingdom is one
that will not be destroyed.

Mark 1:14–15

MINISTRY IN GALILEE

¹⁴ After John was arrested, Jesus went to Galilee, proclaiming the good news of God: ¹⁵ "The time is fulfilled, and the kingdom of God has come near. Repent and believe the good news!"

John 18:36

"My kingdom is not of this world," said Jesus. "If my kingdom were of this world, my servants would fight, so that I wouldn't be handed over to the Jews. But as it is, my kingdom is not from here."

Hebrews 1:3–4

³ The Son is the radiance of God's glory and the exact expression of his nature, sustaining all things by his powerful word. After making purification for sins, he sat down at the right hand of the Majesty on high. ⁴ So he became superior to the angels, just as the name he inherited is more excellent than theirs.

Revelation 11:15

The seventh angel blew his trumpet, and there were loud voices in heaven saying,

The kingdom of the world has become
  the kingdom
of our Lord and of his Christ,
and he will reign forever and ever.

RESPONSE

TIME   DATE

As you respond this week, consider praying about how each day's reading leads you to praise, shapes your perspective on what it means to rejoice, and equips you to encourage those in your community.

WE REJOICE IN GOD'S KINGDOM! WRITE A PRAYER OF GRATITUDE, THANKING HIM FOR GIVING US A FORETASTE OF ETERNITY.

Rejoice

HARK!
THE
HERALD ANGELS

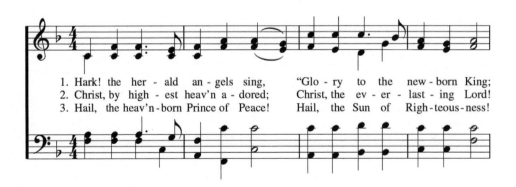

WORDS

Charles Wesley; altered by
George Whitefield

MUSIC

Felix Mendelssohn;
arranged by William H. Cummings

Peace on earth, and mer - cy mild, God and sin - ners rec - on - ciled!"
Late in time be - hold Him come, Off - spring of the Vir - gin's womb:
Light and life to all He brings, Ris'n with heal - ing in His wings.

Joy - ful, all ye na - tions, rise, Join the tri - umph of the skies;
Veiled in flesh the God - head see; Hail th'in - car - nate De - i - ty,
Mild He lays His glo - ry by, Born that man no more may die,

With th'an - gel - ic host pro - claim, "Christ is born in Beth - le - hem!"
Pleased as man with men to dwell, Je - sus, our Em - man - u - el.
Born to raise the sons of earth, Born to give them sec - ond birth.

Hark! the her - ald an - gels sing, "Glo - ry to the new-born King."

WE REJOICE IN

Eternal Life

John 11:17–27

THE RESURRECTION AND THE LIFE

[17] When Jesus arrived, he found that Lazarus had already been in the tomb four days. [18] Bethany was near Jerusalem (less than two miles away). [19] Many of the Jews had come to Martha and Mary to comfort them about their brother.

[20] As soon as Martha heard that Jesus was coming, she went to meet him, but Mary remained seated in the house. [21] Then Martha said to Jesus, "Lord, if you had been here, my brother wouldn't have died. [22] Yet even now I know that whatever you ask from God, God will give you."

[23] "Your brother will rise again," Jesus told her.

[24] Martha said to him, "I know that he will rise again in the resurrection at the last day."

[25] Jesus said to her, "I am the resurrection and the life. The one who believes in me, even if he dies, will live. [26] Everyone who lives and believes in me will never die. Do you believe this?"

[27] "Yes, Lord," she told him, "I believe you are the Messiah, the Son of God, who comes into the world."

John 20:1–18

THE EMPTY TOMB

[1] On the first day of the week Mary Magdalene came to the tomb early, while it was still dark. She saw that the stone had been removed from the tomb. [2] So she went running to Simon Peter and to the other disciple, the one Jesus loved, and said to them, "They've taken the Lord out of the tomb, and we don't know where they've put him!"

[3] At that, Peter and the other disciple went out, heading for the tomb. [4] The two were running together, but the other disciple outran Peter and got to the tomb first. [5] Stooping down, he saw the linen cloths lying there, but he did not go in. [6] Then, following him, Simon Peter also came. He entered the tomb and saw the linen cloths lying there. [7] The

wrapping that had been on his head was not lying with the linen cloths but was folded up in a separate place by itself. [8] The other disciple, who had reached the tomb first, then also went in, saw, and believed. [9] For they did not yet understand the Scripture that he must rise from the dead. [10] Then the disciples returned to the place where they were staying.

MARY MAGDALENE SEES THE RISEN LORD

[11] But Mary stood outside the tomb, crying. As she was crying, she stooped to look into the tomb. [12] She saw two angels in white sitting where Jesus's body had been lying, one at the head and the other at the feet. [13] They said to her, "Woman, why are you crying?"

"Because they've taken away my Lord," she told them, "and I don't know where they've put him."

[14] Having said this, she turned around and saw Jesus standing there, but she did not know it was Jesus. [15] "Woman," Jesus said to her, "why are you crying? Who is it that you're seeking?"

Supposing he was the gardener, she replied, "Sir, if you've carried him away, tell me where you've put him, and I will take him away."

[16] Jesus said to her, "Mary."

Turning around, she said to him in Aramaic, *Rabboni!*"—which means "Teacher."

[17] "Don't cling to me," Jesus told her, "since I have not yet ascended to the Father. But go to my brothers and tell them that I am ascending to my Father and your Father, to my God and your God."

[18] Mary Magdalene went and announced to the disciples, "I have seen the Lord!" And she told them what he had said to her.

Romans 8:34

Who is the one who condemns? Christ Jesus is the one who died, but even more, has been raised; he also is at the right hand of God and intercedes for us.

1 Corinthians 15:12–20, 35–44, 50–57
RESURRECTION ESSENTIAL TO THE FAITH

[12] Now if Christ is proclaimed as raised from the dead, how can some of you say, "There is no resurrection of the dead"? [13] If there is no resurrection of the dead, then not even Christ has been raised; [14] and if Christ has not been raised, then our proclamation is in vain, and so is your faith. [15] Moreover, we are found to be false witnesses about God, because we have testified wrongly about God that he raised up Christ—whom he did not raise up, if in fact the dead are not raised. [16] For if the dead are not raised, not even Christ has been raised. [17] And if Christ has not been raised, your faith is worthless; you are still in your sins. [18] Those, then, who have fallen asleep in Christ have also perished. [19] If we have put our hope in Christ for this life only, we should be pitied more than anyone.

CHRIST'S RESURRECTION GUARANTEES OURS

[20] But as it is, Christ has been raised from the dead, the firstfruits of those who have fallen asleep.

. . .

THE NATURE OF THE RESURRECTION BODY

[35] But someone will ask, "How are the dead raised? What kind of body will they have when they come?" [36] You fool! What you sow does not come to life unless it dies. [37] And as for what you sow—you are not sowing the body that will be, but only a seed, perhaps of wheat or another grain. [38] But God gives it a body as he wants, and to each of the seeds its own body. [39] Not all flesh is the same flesh; there is one flesh for humans, another for animals, another for birds, and another for fish. [40] There are heavenly bodies and earthly bodies, but the splendor of the heavenly bodies is different from that of the earthly ones. [41] There is a splendor of the sun, another of the moon, and another of the stars; in fact, one star differs from another star in splendor. [42] So it is with the resurrection of the dead: Sown in corruption, raised in incorruption; [43] sown in dishonor, raised in glory; sown in weakness, raised in power; [44] sown a natural body, raised a spiritual body. If there is a natural body, there is also a spiritual body.

. . .

[50] What I am saying, brothers and sisters, is this: Flesh and blood cannot inherit the kingdom of God, nor can corruption inherit incorruption. [51] Listen, I am telling you a mystery: We will not all fall asleep, but we will all be changed, [52] in a moment, in the twinkling of an eye, at the last trumpet. For the trumpet will sound, and the dead will be raised incorruptible, and we will be changed. [53] For this corruptible body must be clothed with incorruptibility, and this mortal body must be clothed with immortality. [54] When this corruptible body is clothed with incorruptibility, and this mortal body is clothed with immortality, then the saying that is written will take place:

Death has been swallowed up in victory.
[55] Where, death, is your victory?
Where, death, is your sting?

[56] The sting of death is sin, and the power of sin is the law. [57] But thanks be to God, who gives us the victory through our Lord Jesus Christ!

Colossians 1:18

He is also the head of the body, the church;
he is the beginning,
the firstborn from the dead,
so that he might come to have
first place in everything.

RESPONSE

TIME   DATE

WE REJOICE IN ETERNAL LIFE! WRITE A PRAYER OF GRATITUDE, THANKING HIM
FOR BRINGING ETERNAL LIFE THROUGH HIS RESURRECTION.

Rejoice

2024 YEAR IN REVIEW

Use the following prompts to reflect on the past year.

A VERSE OR PASSAGE OF SCRIPTURE THAT MEANT A LOT TO ME THIS YEAR:

_____

_____

_____

_____

_____

_____

SOMETHING GOD TAUGHT ME ABOUT HIMSELF:

SOMETHING GOD TAUGHT ME ABOUT MYSELF:

WHERE I HAVE SEEN GOD GROW MY RELATIONSHIP WITH HIM:

AN UNEXPECTED DELIGHT:

AN UNEXPECTED SORROW:

A PRAYER TO CLOSE

2 0 2 4 _____

_____

_____

_____

_____

_____

_____

MY PRAYER FOR

2 0 2 5 _____

_____

_____

_____

_____

_____

_____

WE **REJOICE** IN JESUS'S

DAY
32

WEEK
05

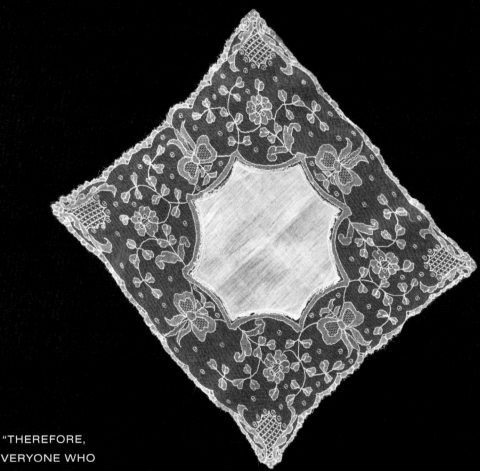

"THEREFORE,
EVERYONE WHO
HEARS THESE
WORDS OF MINE
AND ACTS ON THEM
WILL BE LIKE A
WISE MAN WHO
BUILT HIS HOUSE
ON THE ROCK."

MATTHEW 7:24

Instruction

Matthew 7:13–29

ENTERING THE KINGDOM

¹³ "Enter through the narrow gate. For the gate is wide and the road broad that leads to destruction, and there are many who go through it. ¹⁴ How narrow is the gate and difficult the road that leads to life, and few find it.

¹⁵ "Be on your guard against false prophets who come to you in sheep's clothing but inwardly are ravaging wolves. ¹⁶ You'll recognize them by their fruit. Are grapes gathered from thornbushes or figs from thistles? ¹⁷ In the same way, every good tree produces good fruit, but a bad tree produces bad fruit. ¹⁸ A good tree can't produce bad fruit; neither can a bad tree produce good fruit. ¹⁹ Every tree that doesn't produce good fruit is cut down and thrown into the fire. ²⁰ So you'll recognize them by their fruit.

²¹ "Not everyone who says to me, 'Lord, Lord,' will enter the kingdom of heaven, but only the one who does the will of my Father in heaven. ²² On that day many will say to me, 'Lord, Lord, didn't we prophesy in your name, drive out demons in your name, and do many miracles in your name?' ²³ Then I will announce to them, 'I never knew you. Depart from me, you lawbreakers!'

THE TWO FOUNDATIONS

²⁴ "Therefore, everyone who hears these words of mine and acts on them will be like a wise man who built his house on the rock. ²⁵ The rain fell, the rivers rose, and the winds blew and pounded that house. Yet it didn't collapse, because its foundation was on the rock. ²⁶ But everyone who hears these words of mine and doesn't act on them will be like a foolish man who built his house on the sand. ²⁷ The rain fell, the rivers rose, the winds blew and pounded that house, and it collapsed. It collapsed with a great crash."

²⁸ When Jesus had finished saying these things, the crowds were astonished at his teaching, ²⁹ because he was teaching them like one who had authority, and not like their scribes.

Matthew 22:34–40

THE PRIMARY COMMANDS

³⁴ When the Pharisees heard that he had silenced the Sadducees, they came together. ³⁵ And one of them, an expert in the law, asked a question to test him: ³⁶ "Teacher, which command in the law is the greatest?"

³⁷ He said to him, "Love the Lord your God with all your heart, with all your soul, and with all your mind. ³⁸ This is the greatest and most important command. ³⁹ The second is like it: Love your neighbor as yourself. ⁴⁰ All the Law and the Prophets depend on these two commands."

1 Peter 2:21–25

[21] For you were called to this, because Christ also suffered for you,

leaving you an example, that you should follow in his steps.

[22] He did not commit sin, and no deceit was found in his mouth; [23] when he was insulted, he did not insult in return; when he suffered, he did not threaten but entrusted himself to the one who judges justly. [24] He himself bore our sins in his body on the tree; so that, having died to sins, we might live for righteousness. By his wounds you have been healed. [25] For you were like sheep going astray, but you have now returned to the Shepherd and Overseer of your souls.

RESPONSE

TIME   DATE

WE REJOICE IN JESUS'S INSTRUCTION! WRITE A PRAYER
OF GRATITUDE, THANKING HIM FOR TEACHING US HOW TO LIVE.

Rejoice

WE REJOICE IN THE

Holy Spirit

John 14:18–26

THE FATHER, THE SON, AND THE HOLY SPIRIT

[18] "I will not leave you as orphans; I am coming to you. [19] In a little while the world will no longer see me, but you will see me. Because I live, you will live too. [20] On that day you will know that I am in my Father, you are in me, and I am in you. [21] The one who has my commands and keeps them is the one who loves me. And the one who loves me will be loved by my Father. I also will love him and will reveal myself to him."

[22] Judas (not Iscariot) said to him, "Lord, how is it you're going to reveal yourself to us and not to the world?"

[23] Jesus answered, "If anyone loves me, he will keep my word. My Father will love him, and we will come to him and make our home with him. [24] The one who doesn't love me will not keep my words. The word that you hear is not mine but is from the Father who sent me.

[25] "I have spoken these things to you while I remain with you. [26] But the Counselor, the Holy Spirit, whom the Father will send in my name, will teach you all things and remind you of everything I have told you."

John 15:25–27

[25] "But this happened so that the statement written in their law might be fulfilled: They hated me for no reason.

THE COUNSELOR'S MINISTRY

[26] "When the Counselor comes, the one I will send to you from the Father—the Spirit of truth who proceeds from the Father—he will testify about me. [27] You also will testify, because you have been with me from the beginning."

John 16:1–15

[1] "I have told you these things to keep you from stumbling. [2] They will ban you from the synagogues. In fact, a time is coming when anyone who kills you will think he is offering service to God. [3] They will do these things because they haven't known the Father or me. [4] But I have told you these things so that when their time comes you will remember I told them to you. I didn't tell you these things from the beginning, because I was with you. [5] But now I am going away to him who sent me, and not one of you asks me, 'Where are you going?' [6] Yet, because I have spoken these things to you, sorrow has filled your heart. [7] Nevertheless,

I am telling you the truth. It is for your benefit that I go away, because if I don't go away the Counselor will not come to you. If I go, I will send him to you. [8] When he comes, he will convict the world about sin, righteousness, and judgment: [9] About sin, because they do not believe in me; [10] about righteousness, because I am going to the Father and you will no longer see me; [11] and about judgment, because the ruler of this world has been judged.

[12] "I still have many things to tell you, but you can't bear them now.

[13] When the Spirit of truth comes, he will guide you into all the truth. For he will not speak on his own, but he will speak whatever he hears. He will also declare to you what is to come.

[14] He will glorify me, because he will take from what is mine and declare it to you. [15] Everything the Father has is mine. This is why I told you that he takes from what is mine and will declare it to you."

Acts 1:1–11

PROLOGUE

[1] I wrote the first narrative, Theophilus, about all that Jesus began to do and teach [2] until the day he was taken up, after he had given instructions through the Holy Spirit to the apostles he had chosen. [3] After he had suffered, he also presented himself alive to them by many convincing proofs, appearing to them over a period of forty days and speaking about the kingdom of God.

THE HOLY SPIRIT PROMISED

[4] While he was with them, he commanded them not to leave Jerusalem, but to wait for the Father's promise. "Which," he said, "you have heard me speak about; [5] for John baptized with water, but you will be baptized with the Holy Spirit in a few days."

[6] So when they had come together, they asked him, "Lord, are you restoring the kingdom to Israel at this time?"

[7] He said to them, "It is not for you to know times or periods that the Father has set by his own authority. [8] But you will receive power when the Holy Spirit has come on you, and you will be my witnesses in Jerusalem, in all Judea and Samaria, and to the ends of the earth."

NOTES

THE ASCENSION

[9] After he had said this, he was taken up as they were watching, and a cloud took him out of their sight. [10] While he was going, they were gazing into heaven, and suddenly two men in white clothes stood by them. [11] They said, "Men of Galilee, why do you stand looking up into heaven? This same Jesus, who has been taken from you into heaven, will come in the same way that you have seen him going into heaven."

DAY
33

RESPONSE

TIME

DATE

WE REJOICE IN THE HOLY SPIRIT! WRITE A PRAYER OF GRATITUDE,
THANKING THE SPIRIT FOR DWELLING IN YOU.

Rejoice

WE *Rejoice* IN NEW CREATION

DAY

34

WEEK

05

The one seated on the throne said,
"Look, I am making everything new."

Revelation 21:5

Romans 8:18–30

FROM GROANS TO GLORY

[18] For I consider that the sufferings of this present time are not worth comparing with the glory that is going to be revealed to us. [19] For the creation eagerly waits with anticipation for God's sons to be revealed. [20] For the creation was subjected to futility—not willingly, but because of him who subjected it—in the hope [21] that the creation itself will also be set free from the bondage to decay into the glorious freedom of God's children. [22] For we know that the whole creation has been groaning together with labor pains until now. [23] Not only that, but we ourselves who have the Spirit as the firstfruits—we also groan within ourselves, eagerly waiting for adoption, the redemption of our bodies. [24] Now in this hope we were saved, but hope that is seen is not hope, because who hopes for what he sees? [25] Now if we hope for what we do not see, we eagerly wait for it with patience.

[26] In the same way the Spirit also helps us in our weakness, because we do not know what to pray for as we should, but the Spirit himself intercedes for us with inexpressible groanings. [27] And he who searches our hearts knows the mind of the Spirit, because he intercedes for the saints according to the will of God.

[28] We know that all things work together for the good of those who love God, who are called according to his purpose. [29] For those he foreknew he also predestined to be conformed to the image of his Son, so that he would be the firstborn among many brothers and sisters. [30] And those he predestined, he also called; and those he called, he also justified; and those he justified, he also glorified.

2 Corinthians 5:16–17

[16] From now on, then, we do not know anyone from a worldly perspective. Even if we have known Christ from a worldly perspective, yet now we no longer know him in this way.

[17] **Therefore, if anyone is in Christ, he is a new creation; the old has passed away, and see, the new has come!**

Revelation 21:1–2, 5–7

THE NEW CREATION

[1] Then I saw a new heaven and a new earth; for the first heaven and the first earth had passed away, and the sea was no more. [2] I also saw the holy city, the new Jerusalem, coming down out of heaven from God, prepared like a bride adorned for her husband.

…

[5] Then the one seated on the throne said, "Look, I am making everything new." He also said, "Write, because these words are faithful and true." [6] Then he said to me, "It is done! I am the Alpha and the Omega, the beginning and the end. I will freely give to the thirsty from the spring of the water of life. [7] The one who conquers will inherit these things, and I will be his God, and he will be my son."

Revelation 22:1–5

THE SOURCE OF LIFE

[1] Then he showed me the river of the water of life, clear as crystal, flowing from the throne of God and of the Lamb [2] down the middle of the city's main street. The tree of life was on each side of the river, bearing twelve kinds of fruit, producing its fruit every month. The leaves of the tree are for healing the nations, [3] and there will no longer be any curse. The throne of God and of the Lamb will be in the city, and his servants will worship him. [4] They will see his face, and his name will be on their foreheads. [5] Night will be no more; people will not need the light of a lamp or the light of the sun, because the Lord God will give them light, and they will reign forever and ever.

RESPONSE

TIME   DATE

WE REJOICE IN NEW CREATION! WRITE A PRAYER OF GRATITUDE,
THANKING HIM FOR COMING TO MAKE EVERYTHING NEW.

Rejoice

DAY 35

GRACE *Day*

TAKE THIS DAY TO CATCH UP ON
YOUR READING, PRAY, AND REST
IN THE PRESENCE OF THE LORD.

"WILL NOT LEAVE YOU AS ORPHANS; I AM COMING TO YOU."

JOHN 14:18

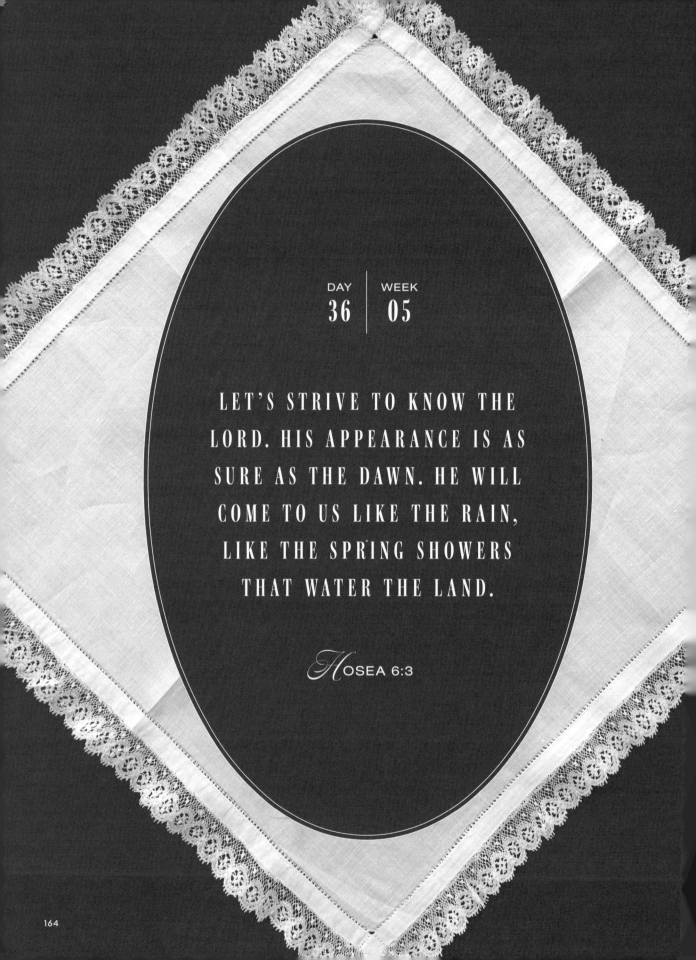

DAY | WEEK
36 | 05

LET'S STRIVE TO KNOW THE
LORD. HIS APPEARANCE IS AS
SURE AS THE DAWN. HE WILL
COME TO US LIKE THE RAIN,
LIKE THE SPRING SHOWERS
THAT WATER THE LAND.

Hosea 6:3

THE
SECOND SUNDAY
OF
CHRISTMASTIDE

As our Advent study and the Christmas season draw to a close,
we celebrate in word and in deed, thanking Jesus for all He has
done and the hope He gives us in the promise of His return.

FOR THE RECORD

Advent 2024

SOMETHING NEW I LEARNED ABOUT
GOD DURING THIS STUDY:

_____

_____

_____

_____

_____

_____

_____

MY FAVORITE READING DAY OR
SCRIPTURE FROM THIS STUDY:

_____

_____

_____

_____

_____

_____

_____

TAKE NOTE OF WHERE YOU FOUND HOPE, PEACE, JOY, AND LOVE THIS ADVENT SEASON.

HOPE	PEACE	JOY	LOVE

BEYOND THIS ADVENT SEASON, HOW CAN I REJOICE
IN WHAT JESUS IS DOING IN MY LIFE AND THE WORLD
AROUND ME?

_____

_____

_____

_____

_____

WHAT DID I LEARN IN THIS ADVENT STUDY THAT I
WANT TO SHARE WITH SOMEONE ELSE?

_____

_____

_____

_____

_____

Tips for Memorizing Scripture

At She Reads Truth, we believe Scripture memorization is an important discipline in your walk with God. Committing God's Truth to memory means we carry it with us and we can minister to others wherever we go.

STUDY IT

Study the passage in its biblical context, and ask yourself a few questions before you begin to memorize it: What does this passage say? What does it mean? How would I say this in my own words? What does it teach me about God? Understanding what the passage means helps you know why it is important to carry it with you wherever you go.

Break the passage into smaller sections, memorizing a phrase at a time.

PRAY IT

Use the passage you are memorizing as a prompt for prayer.

WRITE IT

Dedicate a notebook to Scripture memorization, and write the passage over and over again.

Diagram the passage after you write it out. Place a square around the verbs, underline the nouns, and circle any adjectives or adverbs. Say the passage aloud several times, emphasizing the verbs as you repeat it. Then do the same thing again with the nouns, then the adjectives and adverbs.

Write out the first letter of each word in the passage somewhere you can reference it throughout the week as you work on your memorization.

Use a whiteboard to write out the passage. Erase a few words at a time as you continue to repeat it aloud. Keep erasing parts of the passage until you have it all committed to memory.

CREATE

If you can, make up a tune for the passage to sing as you go about your day, or try singing it to the tune of a favorite song.

Sketch the passage, visualizing what each phrase would look like in the form of a picture. Or try using calligraphy or altering the style of your handwriting as you write it out.

Use hand signals or signs to come up with associations for each word or phrase and repeat the movements as you practice.

SAY IT

Repeat the passage out loud to yourself as you are going through the rhythm of your day—getting ready, pouring your coffee, waiting in traffic, or making dinner.

Listen to the passage read aloud to you.

Record a voice memo on your phone, and listen to it throughout the day or play it on an audio Bible.

SHARE IT

Memorize the passage with a friend, family member, or mentor. Spontaneously challenge each other to recite the passage, or pick a time to review your passage and practice saying it from memory together.

Send the passage as an encouraging text to a friend, testing yourself as you type to see how much you have memorized so far.

KEEP AT IT!

Set reminders on your phone to prompt you to practice your passage.

Purchase a She Reads Truth Scripture Card Set, or keep a stack of note cards with Scripture you are memorizing by your bed. Practice reciting what you've memorized previously before you go to sleep, ending with the passages you are currently learning. If you wake up in the middle of the night, review them again instead of grabbing your phone. Read them out loud before you get out of bed in the morning.

CSB BOOK ABBREVIATIONS

OLD TESTAMENT

GN Genesis	**JB** Job	**HAB** Habakkuk	**PHP** Philippians
EX Exodus	**PS** Psalms	**ZPH** Zephaniah	**COL** Colossians
LV Leviticus	**PR** Proverbs	**HG** Haggai	**1TH** 1 Thessalonians
NM Numbers	**EC** Ecclesiastes	**ZCH** Zechariah	**2TH** 2 Thessalonians
DT Deuteronomy	**SG** Song of Solomon	**MAL** Malachi	**1TM** 1 Timothy
JOS Joshua	**IS** Isaiah		**2TM** 2 Timothy
JDG Judges	**JR** Jeremiah	### NEW TESTAMENT	**TI** Titus
RU Ruth	**LM** Lamentations	**MT** Matthew	**PHM** Philemon
1SM 1 Samuel	**EZK** Ezekiel	**MK** Mark	**HEB** Hebrews
2SM 2 Samuel	**DN** Daniel	**LK** Luke	**JMS** James
1KG 1 Kings	**HS** Hosea	**JN** John	**1PT** 1 Peter
2KG 2 Kings	**JL** Joel	**AC** Acts	**2PT** 2 Peter
1CH 1 Chronicles	**AM** Amos	**RM** Romans	**1JN** 1 John
2CH 2 Chronicles	**OB** Obadiah	**1CO** 1 Corinthians	**2JN** 2 John
EZR Ezra	**JNH** Jonah	**2CO** 2 Corinthians	**3JN** 3 John
NEH Nehemiah	**MC** Micah	**GL** Galatians	**JD** Jude
EST Esther	**NAH** Nahum	**EPH** Ephesians	**RV** Revelation

BIBLIOGRAPHY

Thompson, Jeremy. *Lists from Church History.* Faithlife Biblical and Theological Lists. Bellingham: Faithlife, 2022.

Bonhoeffer, Dietrich. *God Is in the Manger: Reflections on Advent and Christmas.* Translated by O. C. Dean Jr. Compiled and edited by Jana Riess. Louisville: Westminster John Knox Press, 2010.

Your Daily Guide to Reading God's Word

AUTOMATICALLY DELIVERED TO YOU EACH AND EVERY MONTH

If you are looking to establish a habit of daily Bible reading or to grow in your knowledge and understanding of Scripture, look no further. Sign up today and receive our latest Daily Reading Guide delivered to your doorstep monthly.